CLASSIC BRIDGE QUOTES

by
JARED JOHNSON

**Published by
Devyn Press, Inc.
Louisville, Kentucky**

Devyn Press, Inc.
151 Thierman Lane
Louisville, KY 40207

ISBN 0-910791-66-X

TABLE OF CONTENTS

INTRODUCTION

Bridge is a fascinating game. Some suggest it was invented in a mental ward in Constantinople. Later as the game grew in popularity and tournaments were held, the quest for partners became paramount, and a new instrument of torture was born — the partnership table.

*— From a speech on the history of
bridge given at the 1981 spring
nationals in Detroit*

Welcome to "Classic Bridge Quotes." A few quick introductory comments and then you can jump right in.

1. Quote sources include books, newspapers, magazines, interviews, and table talk.

2. You may violently disagree with some of the opinions expressed herein. Many of the quotes were specifically chosen for their provocativeness and/or outrageousness. Don't blame me. I didn't say or write these things. With the exception of some of the special features, I'm just the reporter.

3. Various quotes lack attribution. Some were found that way, but in a few cases I simply failed to note the source when I first picked up the quote. Ten years ago I didn't know I'd be turning this material into a book. If you know the source for any quote attributed to "unknown" or "anonymous," please drop the publisher a line.

4. Occasionally explanatory material accompanies a quote to place it in context. Sometimes not. Please keep in mind that some quotes were surely made tongue-in-cheek (at least one hopes they were).

5. A few quotes were deliberately taken out of context. They were not originally meant to apply to bridge, but the general sentiments expressed were so apropos, I had to include them.

6. If you have a favorite quote, send it in for use in a future edition of "Classic Bridge Quotes."

P.S.

My thanks to Randall Baron for the following items that appear in the book: Movies with "Bridge" in the Title, 25 Bridge Terms with Sexual Connotations, 14 Famous Athletes Who Should Be Bridge Players, 14 Bridge Coups, Famous Bridge Personalities, All-Royalty Bridge Team, Royal Family Members, All-Funeral Bridge Team, Bridge-Playing Cities (Population), the Men-of-the-Cloth Bridge Team, All-World Bridge Team, Occupation Bridge Team, and All-Animal Bridge Team.

ADDICTION (BRIDGE AS AN)

There has never been an addiction with the grip of bridge, unless it be alcohol, and, of the two, bridge is perhaps the stronger. One knows reformed alcoholics, but who knows any reformed bridge players?

— *Jack Olsen*

Once you're hooked, it's like a disease.

— *30-year tournament player*

Contract bridge is a disease, all right. It is malignant and contagious — prevalent in all large cities and most small towns. Practically everybody has it, and virtually nobody recovers.

— *Unknown*

Bridge is not merely a game, as the more naive of us had thought, but an institution, a neurosis, a compulsion, an obsession, a powder keg, a force for peace, a prime cause of evil, and several dozen other things.

— *Charles Goren*

I remember so many people who all but lived for bridge, who would almost have curled up and withered away if they hadn't been able to play. Most of them found it difficult even to express themselves in non-bridge terms away from the table. There was a young man who introduced himself to me and said he was from Sulligent, Alabama. "Sulligent, Alabama?" I said. "How big is Sulligent?" "Oh," he said, "about four tables."

— *Charles Goren*

And I remember a man who was playing in a tournament far from home when he received word that his wife had died. The next available train was six hours later, and if you don't know what that man did for the next six hours, then you don't know bridge players.

— *Charles Goren*

Another group of people use bridge much as other people use liquor or narcotics, as a way to escape unpleasant realities. Bridge has an advantage over liquor and narcotics in that there is no hangover. Also, if the addict cannot obtain the necessary supply of bridge games, the withdrawal symptoms are not as severe.
— *Richard Powell, "Tickets to the Devil"*

Of the most common addictions — tobacco, alcohol, drugs — bridge is clearly the most socially acceptable.
— *Paul Burka*

When an amusement degenerates into a passion, it becomes a menace.
— *Unknown*

People live for bridge, and their souls are wilting away under this monstrous obsession.
— *Unknown*

Bridge, because of its tendency to encourage prolonged smoking and its deadly immobility, is probably the most dangerous game played in England now.
— *Unknown*

I suppose the bridge club can be regarded as a pleasant form of lunacy . . . The question of whether a man soaked in bridge is more of a total social loss than a man obsessed by some other compulsion . . . is a point too philosopical to be unraveled here.
— *Robert Heilbroner*

Movies With BRIDGE In The Title

1. The Bridge (German, 1959)
2. The Bridge at Remagen (US, 1969)
3. Bridge of San Luis Rey (US, 1944)
4. The Bridge on the River Kwai (British, 1957)
5. Bridge to the Sun (US, 1961)
6. The Bridge at Toko-Ri (US, 1954)

Bridge GRIPS you. Many games provide you with fun, but bridge GRIPS you. It exercises your mind. Your mind can rust, you know, but bridge prevents the rust from forming. Bridge is my passion.

— *Omar Sharif*

Bridge is more addictive than anything I have ever known.

— *Grant Baze*

Is it an obsession? God, yes. All the better players have obsessive personalities. It's been said that when you come out of a championship bridge game, you can be more mentally fatigued than a brain surgeon. It's an intense game and you get hooked on that. For me, bridge is like heroin. I had to get completely off it. I can't just cut down. I have to get completely away from it.

— *Grant Baze*

Bridge is a kind of benign addiction for a lot of people.

— *Dr. Harold Rockaway*

How can a game played with 52 pieces of pasteboard have such potential for wreaking havoc in our social encounters?

— *Ron Klinger*

What is more important, bridge or life? For the truly dedicated bridge player, there is only one answer. Reincarnation may guarantee another life later, but bridge is here and now. For the true devotee, bridge takes precedence over almost everything.

— *Ron Klinger*

Today the really fanatical master-pointer, particularly if he lives in a city, will play in a tournament every night of his life in unremitting greed for pieces of paper which will, probably erroneously, inform the world that he is a better player than his next-door neighbor.

— *Rex Mackey*

9

We are fanatics, a bunch of crazy people. It's like a drug. You get hooked and you can't live without it. You just keep coming back for more.

— Gary King

It's a way of life — I can't imagine being happy without it.

— Robert Hamman

The game is basically addictive.

— Ron Andersen, who was on the road almost constantly in 1983 setting a record to that date of 2,994 masterpoints earned in a single year

---

25 BRIDGE Terms With Sexual Connotations

1. Avoidance
2. Come-On
3. Concession
4. Discourage
   (Encourage)
5. Discovery Play
6. Down (Go Down)
7. Elopement
8. End Play
9. Entry
10. Exit
11. Forcing
12. Laydown
13. Make
14. Trick
15. 2 Over 1
16. Peter
17. Pump
18. Pick Up
19. Ride
20. Rubber
21. Strip
22. Squeeze
23. Unprotected
24. Vulnerable
25. Honor

AGE

There are exceptions (I know great players who are in their 70's) but bridge champions usually peak in their late 30's.

— *Alan Sontag*

It's not the skill that drops off with age, it's the drive, the killer instinct . . . and when a man isn't primed to kill he makes mistakes.

— *Unknown*

Bridge is the only game or sport that people can — and do — play from the age of ten to the age of one hundred.

— *Alan Truscott*

Young man! You do not play whist? What a sad old age you reserve for yourself.

— *Talleyrand*

Bridge is a great comfort in your old age. It also helps you get there faster.

— *Unknown sage*

ARGUMENTS

Why is it that the bridge table so frequently becomes a regular battlefield? Is it because the game attracts people who are naturally quarrelsome, or does the game incite peace-loving players to roar and argue?

— *Frank Perkins*

We believe that contract is particularly attractive to people with a scrappy disposition.

— *Frank Perkins*

The game of contract bridge creates more arguments than any other card game in history. I believe this is part of the game's fascination.

— *Charles Goren*

11

BAD BEHAVIOR

The ACBL is dedicated to the fiction that bridge is a social pastime played by ladies and gentlemen for relaxation.
— *Stanley Frank*

Four bridge players grouped around a table make a foursome. They can also make a lousy evening.
— *Joe James*

Whist led to bridge-whist, which led to auction bridge, which led to contract bridge, which led to murder, divorce, suicide, mayhem and other social evils.
— *Jack Olsen*

Bridge players are mean, sarcastic and gleeful in victory.
— *Catherine Ford*

Mr. (Harry) Meacham had been dealt what seemed like an interminable run of indifferent cards and announced that he would shoot the next man who dealt him a bad hand. It happened to be his deal, and having dealt himself a yarborough he kept his promise and shot himself through the head.
— *Rex Mackey*

Has there ever been a worthwhile scandal at dominoes or checkers, or a murder of note at chess? Of course not. But there have been scandals galore at bridge, several murders, at least one suicide and a number of divorces.
— *Victor Mollo*

One gets use to abuse. It's waiting for it that is so trying.
— *Rueful Rabbit*

At bridge, the bad apples are the ones who can't shake off a lurking feeling of inadequacy. To compensate, they are inclined to berate their partner and-or the opponents and belittle their efforts.
— *Frank Stewart*

My experience suggests that it's a whole lot easier to beat somebody who likes you than somebody who wants to send you home in a box. So I'd be staying on good terms with the world if I were you.

— *Frank Stewart*

Most of the complaints about bridge boil down to this, that it is sometimes played by the wrong people. Too much liquor brings out your true nature, whatever that may be; and so does a bad bid, a disastrous takeout, a stupid play by your partner. People who crack under such a strain would crack under whatever strain might be imposed on them, and I do not see that bridge can be blamed for it.

— *Elmer Davis*

Friendly people are seldom good players.

— *Mike Lawrence*

"What happens if . . .," among tournament players is a phrase that generally means: "You idiot, why didn't you . . .?"

— *Terence Reese*

Since the average person's small supply of politeness must last him all his life, he can't afford to waste it on bridge partners.

— *Alfred Sheinwold*

I believe that the problem is not so much conventions, but the many socially retarded individuals that exist and thrive in the world of bridge today.

— *Letter to The Contract Bridge Bulletin on problems facing the growth of bridge*

My experience suggests that it's a lot easier to beat opponents who like you than those who want to destroy you. If you antagonize your opponents, many of them will react by resolving firmly to send you to the next table with a fishhook in your gills.

— *Frank Stewart*

According to the history of playing cards section of the *Official Encyclopedia of Bridge*, the earliest known cards were used in China about 979 A.D. The pack was divided into four suits of 14 cards each and was used as paper money as well.

Supposedly, a Venetian (possibly Niccolo Polo or his more famous son, Marco) carried cards from China to his native city, the first place in Europe where they were known.

Bridge is essentially a social game, but unfortunately it attracts a substantial number of antisocial people.

— *Alan Truscott*

The nuisance is prevalent at every level — in major tournaments — in small clubs, and in private homes. The menace is perhaps worst in a domestic game, since there is no escape.

— *Unknown*

The persons who feel it necessary to conclude each hand with a magisterial correction of their partners (and their opponents as well) have no place at the bridge table, or anywhere else where they might come into contact with civilized beings.

— *Elmer Davis in "Harper's"*
50 years ago

(There is) a special kind of demon — the tyrant. The bridge tyrant is a person who plays the game for the very opposite of the normal reasons. It has never occurred to him that bridge is fun, or is supposed to be. They are not there to see what is right and enjoy it, but to see what is wrong and to fume about it. And this is exactly why the partner-tyrant came to the bridge club to play. There is nothing more corrosive to pleasant, happy bridge than one of these rotten apples. You can be playing with two other players who are jollity and joy personified, but if there is a single tyrant in the group, the whole game will take its character from him. And his partner's life will be undiluted misery.

— *Charles Goren*

In no other game is there such spite, petty bickering, and jealousy.

— Unknown

"A nice quiet game" is the ideal of the management of every bridge club. There are no loud voices to disturb the fighting at the other tables, and nobody has his feelings hurt. But we believe that bridge players like to fight; and after a quarrel, the whole crowd will be on hand early for the next day's game.

— Frank Perkins

A not surprising aftermath of the Bennett (murder) case was that Mrs. Bennett found it exceedingly difficult to find bridge partners.

— Ron Klinger

We all know the aggressive, bustling type of player who, using what he considers his best tournament tactics, assumes a supremely confident and garrulous manner when pitted against almost any type of adversary. No one has ever quite succeeded in explaining the attitude of such players. Perhaps they entertain the furtive hopes of frightening you by their seeming knowledge and verbosity. Perhaps they are trying, feebly, to rejuvenate the morale of their partners. Perhaps they are just naturally objectionable.

— P. Hal Sims

Another session like tonight's will show Lenz and Jacoby as the world's worst losers. I have never seen so much petty squabbling, unknowing gestures and petty despairs as in tonight's game.

— Josephine Culbertson during the famous Culbertson-Lenz match in 1931

Obscure BRIDGE Term Quiz

1. Bumblepuppy: a. inferior play; b. inferior bidding; c. any fourth asked to fill in; d. one who doesn't know how to play bridge at all. Answer on page 108.

BAD BIDDING

No matter how bad the bidding is, there's usually one combination of the cards that will allow you to make it.
— *Craig Janitschke*

More boards are lost on bad bidding than any other factor.
— *Unknown*

One advantage of bad bidding is that you get practice at playing atrocious contracts.
— *Alfred Sheinwold*

Players who count points and don't take note of distribution are a menace.
— *Terence Reese*

Good bidding makes for dull bridge.
— *Clyde Graham*

Where's the hand you held during the auction?
— *A comment Jan Janitschke has been known to make as dummy hits*

Tragedy is more instructive than triumph. There are more lessons to be drawn from it.
— *Victor Mollo*

It dawned on me that bad bids — that is, bids I wouldn't have made — frequently made good drama. Without them, bridge would be dull, like errorless baseball.
— *Charles Goren*

Why do you make such rotten bids?
— *Sidney Lenz to partner Oswald Jacoby during the Culbertson-Lenz match, 1931-32*

If you think there's any chance of partner not understanding the bid — don't make it!
— *Ken Baikie*

South (after partner's bid): Alert!
East: What's that?
South: I'm requested to further misdescribe my hand.
— *Overheard at the bridge table*

Results are all that count.
— *Ben Carrington on "Dynasty"*

George S. Kaufman expressed the belief that much of the bidding difficulty encountered by the average player could be done away with by seating partners differently. Instead of facing each other they should be allowed to sit side by side on a small bench. This would enable them to look at each other's hand and do away with the need for systems and conventions.

— *Albert Ostrow*

We've all encountered partners for whom a particular bidding sequence has meaning only in the context of the hand they actually hold; like Humpty Dumpty, they maintain that their bidding must show just the hand they were dealt, because, after all, those are the bids made with the cards held.

— *Allan Falk*

Partner, don't place cards in my hand, because I won't have them.

— *Barry Crane*

Playing with Barry (Crane) forced you to become a better declarer, because you were in so many absurd contracts.

— *Gerald Caravelli*

BRIDGE Trivia Quiz

2. What did Mrs. Bennett do to Mr. Bennett during a rubber bridge game?
3. In what year did it happen?
4. What contract did Mr. Bennett butcher?
5. What happened to Mrs. Bennett? Answers on page 108.

BAD CONTRACTS

If you're in the wrong contract, it's tough to salvage much of anything.

— Max Hardy

Few lousy contracts can be overcome by sparkling declarer play.

— Anonymous

You can play or defend like mad but if you are in the wrong contract it won't do you any good.

— Anonymous

A contract is neither good nor bad, but playing makes it so.

— Victor Mollo

---

14 Famous Athletes Who Should Be BRIDGE Players

1. Spectacular BID
2. Abner DOUBLEday
3. Forward PASS
4. Frank PAStore
5. Ken SINGLETON
6. Gene TENACE
7. Bob TRUMPey
8. Red RUFFING
9. Cale YARBOROUGH
10. Rocky BRIDGES
11. Junior BRIDGEMAN
12. Norm CASH
13. Jerry WEST
14. Andy NORTH

BAD LUCK

Harry Meacham of Wilkesboro, North Carolina, got so sick of holding bad hands that he swore he'd kill the next person who dealt him one. On his own next deal he picked up a hand without a face card. He shot himself.

— *Richard Frey*

Seven clubs! I could hardly believe my ears. Here I was defending a vulnerable grand slam with the king-ten of trumps tucked away safely in back of the original club bidder. God isn't an Italian after all. They were certain to go down one, I was going to be a world champion. What a day . . .

— Eddie Kantar in "The Short Life of the King of Clubs," explaining how Giorgio Belladonna (in the 1975 world championships) bid to seven clubs — the ace-queen tight hit in dummy and declarer held jack-sixth. Bye-bye world championship.

Have you ever had the feeling you were about to be catastrophically fixed?

— *Tony Sowter*

I think declarer will play the heart ace and then nothing for ten minutes.

— Edgar Kaplan hosting a vugraph presentation at the 1983 world championships (six hearts was the contract and the trumps broke five-zero)

Have you noticed how many bridge players have a tendency to emphasize their hard luck? It is a distinct form of hypochondria. An ordinary hypochondriac is one who appears to enjoy bad health. A bridge hypochondriac is one who enjoys bad luck. They appear to take a great pride and to derive immense pleasure from the claim that they are "bad holders." It is strange how easy it is to forget good cards.

— *Charles Goren*

Do not believe in, or talk about, luck. Of course, you may have bad luck for weeks or even months on end. But if you regularly lose, you are not the unluckiest player at the table; he is your partner.

— Edward Mayer

Nine out of ten players who attribute their losses to bad cards might emerge winners if they devoted half as much time to improving their game as they do to berating Lady Luck.

— P. Hal Sims

Do not ascribe to bad luck, the result of bad play.

— J. B. Elwell

I must complain the cards are ill-shuffled til I have a good hand.

— Jonathan Swift

If dirt was trumps, what hands you would hold.

— Charles Lamb

BIDDING, DECLARER PLAY, AND DEFENSE (WHICH IS MOST IMPORTANT?)

It is generally agreed that defense is the most difficult part of the game of bridge.

— Victor Mollo

All are crucial, but most swings in expert play are from, in order, bidding, opening lead, defense, declarer play.

— Eric Rodwell

Bidding is most important because it makes declarer play easier if you are playing the right contract.

— Marc Jacobus

Playing a hand can be routine but getting to the right place is more difficult.

— Gaylor Kasle

6. Chicane: a. tricky play; b. a passed out hand; c. a void in trumps; d. a hand dealt after the previous hand was passed out. Answer on page 108.

At the top level, most IMPs will be won or lost in the bidding. Declarer play is rarely a factor.

— *Paul Lewis*

No matter how good you are, playing in the wrong contract won't help you.

— *George Rosenkranz*

Getting to a good contract is all important.

— *Max Hardy*

Frequently, if you are in the right contract, the rest takes care of itself.

— *Martha Beecher*

If you aren't in the proper contract, no matter how well you play, very often it won't help. I believe that in expert competition, you will find more excellent card players than excellent bidders.

— *Norman Kay*

Bridge is definitely a bidder's game.

— *Ron Andersen*

Obviously, it is not of the slightest use to become an expert in one department of the game only.

— *Ben Cohen*

More points are lost in the bidding, both matchpoints or total points, for two reasons: If you don't reach the right contract, good play does little good; if you reach the right contract, best play doesn't often change the result.

— *Richard Frey*

If you can't do all three reasonably well, what difference does it make? You aren't going to win.

— *Anonymous*

BIDS-OUT-OF-TURN

I don't think the opening bids out-of-turn have been fully explored in the bridge literature.

— *Chuck Henke*

BRIDGE (IN GENERAL)

Bridge is the most entertaining and intelligent card game the wit of man has so far devised.

— *Somerset Maugham*

Undoubtedly, the game is the greatest waster of time and money ever devised by man.

— *Collier's magazine, 1934*

Of all the manifold human contests by which the world finds amusement, the game of contract bridge may well be the most ubiquitous. The British have their cricket; the French love bicycle racing; The Russians are chess fanatics; the Americans call baseball the national game. But *all* nationalities play bridge.

— *Jack Olsen*

We don't have the rough physical contact of hockey, football or basketball, but we have a sport in which social contact is an important part of the enjoyment of the game. Bridge brings players of all ages, both sexes, and most social levels to a common meeting place, the bridge table and 52 cards.

— *Don Oakie*

One ancient Hindu deck included 144 cards, eight suits of 18 cards each. How would you like to try playing bridge with that deck?

In early times (and even today by an unenlightened few), cards were often looked upon as evil, and referred to as the Devil's Picture Book.

Is bridge, in fact, a sport? Yes. It is a sport as brutal and as tough as professional football when it is played on the highest level.

— Ira Corn

The game is infinitely more complex than any other competitive sport.

— Ira Corn

A fierce concentration on a petty end . . . a drunken attempt to escape from realities.

— "The New Republic" many years ago

The effect of this game on blood pressure and the heart must be obvious, for it is even more exciting than poker, almost as exciting as alcohol when taken as a beverage. Some of my friends have told me that they cannot get to sleep after a hard bout at bridge. And it (the game) is vindictive, if for no other reason, because such devices as the "squeeze" and the "endplay" are related in their nature to the rack and the thumbscrew. Competition is a form of warfare, which by militarists may be regarded as good sport, but which is manslaughter in one of its cruelest forms; and nowhere is the spirit of devastating competition more fiercely aroused than in contract bridge. Husbands and wives quarrel, families are sundered, because of mistaken bidding or the fall of the cards. The fact that a king is on the wrong side of the board, and that a finesse therefore fails, may precipitate a tempest. The truth is that contract bridge, as I see it, has brought a distortion of values and a maladjustment of the national life which needs to be remedied. Our best hope, I think, is that the fad will cure itself, or kill itself.

— Silas Bent writing in 1937
that bridge should be abolished

Why has bridge died? Because all the younger talent is interested in sex and electronic games.

— Grant Baze

The most intellectually demanding and rewarding sport on earth . . . one of the most complex and devilish games the human race has managed to devise.

— *Alan Sontag*

Anyone who spends the time to appreciate the subtleties of the game, will be in for a lifetime of enjoyment.

— *Warren Buffett*

One could not imagine (Aristotle) expert at bridge, or at golf, or at any other of the idiotic games at which what are called successful men commonly divert themselves.

— *H. L. Mencken*

Bridge is a game only to the dub. To the man who takes his game seriously, it is torment. Annoyance, impatience, disappointment, rage — the confirmed addict suffers all of these. If he likes bridge enough to play it well, its pleasure vanishes.

— *Geraldine Smith*

---

14 BRIDGE Coups

1. ALCATRAZ
2. BATH
3. DESCHAPELLES
4. DOUBLE
5. EN PASSANT
6. GRAND
7. MERRIMAC
8. MORTON'S FORK
9. PITT
10. ROBERT
11. SCISSORS (Without a Name)
12. SIMPLE
13. TRIPLE
14. VIENNA

The duffer . . . knows nothing but pure satisfaction. He sits down at the table with joy in his heart. He bids by the seat of his pants. He plays the hand with complete disregard for percentages. He defends with no regard for signals. That without a doubt, is the way bridge should be played by the average man — carelessly, gladly, terribly. The advantage — mental and spiritual — which the luck player enjoys over the expert is that he gets a great kick out of one or two good boards. Whereas the expert, when he muffs a couple, decides to drink poison.

— Geraldine Smith

Famous BRIDGE Personalities

1. Neil DIAMOND
2. Legs DIAMOND
3. Sam SPADE
4. HANDel
5. Lloyd BRIDGES
6. DOUBLEmint gum twins
7. DIAMOND Jim Brady
8. Gary HART

An enormous amount of mental energy is expended in this universal craze for bridge with no more tangible result than the exchange of relatively unimportant sums of money. Society as a whole is neither benefited nor damaged by this futile activity. Proficiency at bridge is a sterile excellence, sharpening the mental faculties very one-sidedly, without enriching the soul in any way, fixing and consuming a quantity of intellectual energy that might have been better applied. The most we can say, I think, is that it might have been applied worse.

— Dutch social philosopher, John Huizinga in his 1944 book, "Homo Ludens (A Study of the Play Element in Culture)"

BRIDGE PLAYERS

Friendly people are seldom good players.
— *Mike Lawrence (with tongue-in-cheek, one hopes)*

Scientists used to think that animals were guided by instinct and men by reason, but recent experiments reveal that bridge players also rely more on instinct than on thought. Is it possible that bridge players aren't human?
— *Alfred Sheinwold*

Most people you meet at the bridge table are pleasant enough, but sometimes you're pitted against a fiend in human shape.
— *Alfred Sheinwold*

A pike is a despised fish, greedy but prudent. Making due allowance for the person who takes bridge as casual pastime or well-earned distraction, there is something of the pike about the habitual bridge player.
— *"The New Republic," 1914*

One must remember that bridge players would not be bridge players if they were logical thinkers.
— *Jack Olsen*

You couldn't drag a real thinker to the bridge table with a team of horses.
— *Prof. Harold Swenson*

Many Americans who play bridge have subconscious feelings of guilt about it.
— *Richard Powell*

To play a game well may be a sign of an ill-spent life.
— *Alfred Sheinwold*

For some time as I met more bridge players . . . the belief had slowly been growing that most bridge players were nuts. I guess "obsessed" is the more polite description.

— Joyce Nicholson

Bridge players fall into two categories. Those who become obsessed by the game, and look upon it as a way of life, and those who play it as a more intelligent way of passing their time.

— Joyce Nicholson

The uncharted jungle of American bridge clubs is crawling with predatory flora and fauna.

— Fleur Tamon, "The Houston Post"

The two most common professions associated with bridge are the law and medicine. In the 1950's and 1960's, it was the legal profession that produced more top bridge players than any other. (Today, the top young players more commonly come from the computer programming area.)

— Ron Klinger

Bridge players exist mainly to make life difficult for each other.

— Omar Sharif

All-Royalty BRIDGE Team

1. Randall BARON
2. Ronald CROWN
3. Christopher EARL
4. Brian GRACE
5. Gaylor KASLE
6. J. David KING
7. John KNIGHT
8. Roger LORD
9. Peter RANK
10. Herbert ROYAL

BRIDGE SKILLS

Bridge is above all an analytical game. Confirmation of this theory is found if we examine how the top exponents of the game earn their bread. Few can rely on bridge for a living. Most of the experts have to work, and a surprising number of them are employed in the computer industry as programmers or systems analysts, jobs where they utilize the same skills that they bring to the bridge table. Thus there would seem to be a marked relationship between computer aptitude and card sense. Also well represented in the ranks of the experts are lawyers, doctors and teachers, all professions in which logical analysis is to the fore. There appears to be no special affinity between bridge and mathematics. This is not really surprising since it does not take a mathematical genius to add up to thirteen. There are perhaps as many musicians as mathematicians at the top level.

— *H. W. Kelsey*

The essentials for playing a good game of bridge are to be truthful, clearheaded, and considerate, prudent but not averse to taking a risk, and not to cry over spilt milk. And incidentally those are perhaps also the essentials for playing the more important game of life.

— *Somerset Maugham*

Universal Laws of BRIDGE

- Whatever you bid is wrong.
- When the opponents make a bad bid, it works out well for them. When you make a bad bid, it also works out well for them.
- The probability of a bad trump break increases in direct proportion to how high you have bid, whether you are doubled and whether or not you are vulnerable. Corollory: If you bid game, trumps don't split. If you don't, they do.

The beautiful part of this game is that if you can think, you can play it. There's no competitive thing that you can think of that has fewer physical requirements.

— *Robert Bonomi*

Of the 32 million people in the U. S. who play contract bridge, at least 31 million know practically nothing about the game. In no other field of endeavor are so many smart people so blissfully unaware of their own ignorance. Regardless of the category they belong in, America's 32 million bridge fanatics almost all share one thing; mentally, emotionally and physically they simply are not equipped to play bridge as it should be played.

— *Marshall Smith*

Bridge is a highly emotional game. It is also a game that should be played completely devoid of emotion.

— *Alan Sontag*

The ultimate in bridge is learning to play with poor cards.

— *Chip Martel*

You have to be able to tackle each new problem without worrying about how well or poorly you solved the last one.

— *Peter Pender*

You have to keep playing to maintain a certain level of competency. It's like anything else.

— *Alan Sontag*

It is not the handling of difficult hands that makes the winning player. There aren't enough of them. It is the ability to avoid messing up the easy ones.

— *S. J. Simon*

A technician is a man who knows exactly what to do the moment he has done something else.

— *Peregrine the Penguin (Mollo)*

BRIDGE Trivia Quiz

7. Before he got hooked on bridge, what was Charles Goren's profession? Answer on page 108.
8. What are the three most common hand patterns? Answer on page 109.
9. Which is more likely, that you and your partner hold all the clubs between you or that you and your partner hold no clubs between you? Answer on page 109.

Whist has long been known for its influence upon what is termed the calculating power; and men of the highest order of intellect have been known to take an apparently unaccountable delight in it. Beyond doubt there is nothing of a similar nature so greatly tasking the faculty of analysis . . . proficiency in whist implies capacity for success in all these more important undertakings where mind struggles with mind.

— Edgar Allan Poe from "The Murders in the Rue Morgue"

Some players are great bidders, some great declarers. Others are best on defense. But the players who win most consistently are those who can concentrate under pressure and play up to their potential.

— Matthew Granovetter

There's nothing like talent and diligence. You can achieve terrific results with either attribute and tremendous results with both. There is a third ingredient for success which is useful no matter where your strengths lie. This is: a dignified and confident table manner. Confidence is a tremendous psychological advantage, as anyone who plays cards will tell you. If you act the part of an expert bridge player you will sometimes be able to trick the opponents into believing you are one.

— Matthew Granovetter

Most bridge players prefer consistency in their partners rather than brilliance.

— *Matthew Granovetter*

The greatest attribute for any human endeavor is experience. It takes years to become a truly great bridge player.

— *Matthew Granovetter*

The fact that logic is called for at the bridge table often distresses the players who attend the duplicate merely for a night out on the town. Logic, not high level arithmetic, is the bridge player's most critical tool.

— *Matthew Granovetter*

It's my opinion that any stupe can learn to play contract bridge. As a matter of fact, many do.

— *Milton Ozaki*

One has to be a killer. The days of kid gloves are over.

— *"Journal," 1951*

Would you try to play golf or tennis blindfolded? That does not seem a very intelligent thing to do, but most players do exactly that when they play the hand at contract bridge.

— *Robert Hamman*

Mark my words. Good bidding will ruin bridge. Technique does not lie in obscure percentage chances or in safety plays to guard against a nine-zero split. No sir. Technique in its highest form, as every hog knows, is the art of the impossible.

— *The Hideous Hog*

The successful bridge player must be something of a psychologist. He must play men as well as cards.

— *R. R. Richards*

You need skill and imagination and also need to be a little bit of a con artist.

— *Anonymous*

Being a good bridge player is merely the most rudimentary requirement of duplicate bridge. More important is having the nerves, tenacity and stamina of tautly strung steel wire, plus a natural killer instinct.

— Fleur Tamon, "The Houston Post"

The game itself does not require intellect so much as a certain low cunning . . . and allied to this low cunning is a complete disregard of the qualities of which I spoke above — courtesy, sense of fair play, self-control — which are the attributes of civilized persons. So that a bridge player — while playing bridge, of course — is reduced to the status of a clever animal, with an animal's instinctive reactions to that which displeases it. Bridge fiends are very poor company for the normal (or non-bridge playing) human being.

— "Glasgow Weekly Herald," many years ago

Royal Family Members

Most scholars agree that the court cards of the early French decks represented the following:

KINGS:

Clubs — Alexander the Great, King of Macedonia.
Diamonds — Augustus Caesar, first Roman emperor.
Hearts — Charlemagne, King of France.
Spades — David, King of Israel.

QUEENS:

Clubs — Argine (not a person but an anagram for *regina, queen* in Latin).
Diamonds — Rachel, Old Testament wife of Jacob.
Hearts — Judith, Old Testament widow who killed the Assyrian general Holofernes.
Spades — Pallas Athena, Greek goddess of war and wisdom.

JACKS:

Clubs — Lancelot, knight of the court of King Arthur.
Diamonds — Roland, one of Charlemagne's 12 peers of France.
Hearts — La Hire, French commander in the Hundred Years War and loyal companion of Joan of Arc.
Spades — Ogier, another of Charlemagne's peers.

The sum of all technical knowledge cannot make a master contract player.

— *Ely Culbertson*

Happily bridge is an art, not a science.

— *Victor Mollo*

A player may know everything about bridge technique, but if he is lacking in bridge psychology or knowledge of the personal equation, he cannot succeed.

— *Ely Culbertson*

A knowledge of the mechanics will suffice to put a player in a commanding position in the post-mortem. To become a member of the upper crust calls for more, much more. Resilience, imagination, occasional flashes of inspiration, these are the hallmarks of quality. And this transcends the realm of science.

— *Victor Mollo*

Technique will help us up to a point. After that, psychology should be our guide. Bridge is a contest between humans never between cardinal points, and the human element transcends, and will always transcend, all others.

— *Victor Mollo*

I play men, not cards.

— *Ely Culbertson*

The difference between genius and stupidity is that genius has its limits.

— *Anonymous*

You have to be smart enough to understand the game, but dumb enough to think it's important.

— *Zeke Jabbour, responding to a kibitzer's inquiry about the complexity of the game*

I have always been fascinated by the bizarre world of cards. It was a world of pure power where rewards and punishments were meted out immediately. A deck of cards was built like the purest of hierarchies with every card master to those below it and a lackey to those above it. And there were 'masses' — long suits — which always asserted themselves in the end, triumphing over the kings and aces. In bridge every play was in itself a problem of force and timing. And the inexorable rhythm of the law of probabilities dominated the fall of the cards like the beating of a tom-tom. I was at home in this unique world of cards, and I seldom lost.

— Ely Culbertson comparing cards
and politics

If bridge brains were good for anything but bridge, you might expect this nation to be ruled by its tournament stars. I cannot recall that any of them has been conspicuously successful at anything but bridge.

— Elmer Davis

The strain of hours at the table with little relief from problems and anxieties must be worse than the strain of a long-distance runner. There should be practices, exercises, psychological techniques for this mental sport. The enormous potential for great thinking still remains untapped in even the best players.

— Matthew Granovetter

With more than 8,600,000,000 permutations of cards, nobody can play bridge perfectly. Perfection (if possible) would remove all interest in the game.

— George Beynon

Obscure BRIDGE Term Quiz

10. Devil's bedposts: a. the four of clubs; b. the four of spades; c. the two of clubs; d. the two of spades. Answer on page 109.

Blind adherence to bridge maxims is losing strategy.

— *Robert Ewen*

Success at bridge appears, in fact, to require a certain type of mind — a mind capable of assembling a wide range of data, analysing it and drawing the correct conclusions. It is the type of mind possessed by crossword enthusiasts, puzzle solvers and cipher experts. Bridge is above all, an analytical game.

— *Hugh Kelsey*

Superior bridge is often largely the result of superior experience.

— *Albert Ostrow*

BRIDGE WRITERS

Are bridge writers really necessary? A friend of mine holds the view that we are charlatans, presenting simple solutions to problems which, at the table, are far from simple.

— *Hugh Kelsey*

BUTCHERS

If you're lucky, you know one bridge player in whom you have the utmost confidence. You can let him play the hand because if there is one way to throw the contract away, he will surely find it.

— *Alfred Sheinwold*

It's very discouraging to start a hand with 12 tricks and wind up with only 10.

— *Alfred Sheinwold*

CARDS

My mother thought that cards were part of the devil and shouldn't be touched.

— *Oswald Jacoby*

CARD COMBINATIONS

No bridge book has ever attempted to present a solution to all the situations which may arise. None ever will. There are 635,013,559,600 possible combinations of the cards, and, if you were to sit and deal out a new hand every three minutes, eight hours a day, six days a week, 52 weeks a year, it would take 12,644,630 years, 9 months, 3 weeks and 5 days before the hands began to repeat themselves.
— *Milton Ozaki*

CARD SENSE

Bridge is pretty much a microcosm of life. I think the key factor in playing good bridge is card sense. That's something you can't learn. That's something you're born with.
— *Tannah Hirsch*

Card sense is when it's technically right to do something, the little man that sits on my shoulder or anyone else's shoulder says, "Don't do that." And you say to yourself, "Well, wait a minute, that's the right way to play." And he says, "Yeah, but you don't wanna play that way." That instinct is card sense. It's almost an ability to feel where the cards are. It's something that you can't buy, you can't find; you're born with. The ability to do the right thing at the wrong time or really to do the wrong thing at the right time.
— *Barry Crane*

Universal Laws of BRIDGE

- Kings lie behind aces when you hold the aces. Aces lie behind kings when you hold the kings.
- If you have contracted to take "x" number of tricks, you will take "x-1."

Mr. Crane, I have watched you for 51 deals, and you have bid on every one of them.

— A kibitzer to Barry Crane

It's an old saying I use — it's becoming an adage for me — that I came out of the womb shuffling and dealing.

— Barry Crane

My trophies from the cinema are lined up, hidden in corners, lost, objects of little value in my eyes; I have been known to leave them behind in hotel rooms. Yet the smallest bridge cup is a treasure.

— Omar Sharif

He fooled 200 million people for years. Why not two opponents at the bridge table?

— A tournament bridge player speculating on how good a bridge player Richard Nixon would have made

Stripped of all offices, he was excoriated in pamphlets and posters of the Red Guard for not only being a "capitalist roader" and a "revolutionist" and "a demon" but also for succumbing to sybaritic bourgeois pleasures such as bridge, mah-jongg and multi-course banquets.

— "Look" magazine on Chinese leader Deng-Ziao-Ping, circa 1966 when he was out of power

They don't tip. They come to Las Vegas with the Ten Commandments and a $10 bill. When they leave, neither has been broken.

— Bill Cosby at the 1979 Summer North American Championships in Las Vegas, commenting on the rumor that bridge players are cheapskates.

I know I was a riverboat gambler in another life.

— Barry Crane

CHESS (VS. BRIDGE)

Chess players glorify their game for being totally free of luck. Bah! If you don't want to deal with luck, go out and start an insurance company. Bridge is a game; games are supposed to have luck. Though in the long run, bridge is a game of percentages, on any particular hand, it may pay to defy them. This is only a small part of the psychological aspect of bridge; of much greater significance is the fact that the game is played by partners, not individuals. In chess, if you lose, YOU lose. Chess players see this as a virtue, but, in fact, bridge is more demanding. It offers the opportunity to blame someone else for your own sins and this makes the game, for those who yield to the temptation much harder to master.

— *Paul Burka in September, 1978*
"Texas Monthly"

Some persons say chess is the ultimate game, but there are only 64 squares. Chess possibilities may be exhausted someday. What happens in chess today? You may get one innovation every year or two. That's not the case in bridge. Every time you deal there's something new — there's something different.   — *Omar Sharif*

As an intellectual pastime, contract bridge is already considered by many to be superior to chess.

— *Fred Karpin in 1960*

Has it not been shown that whist, as a game, possesses claims to be ranked above chess? Has it not been shown that whist is calculated to promote to the utmost the amusement and relaxation of those employed? The game of whist may fairly be said to combine the means of innocent recreation, of healthy excitement, and of appropriate mental exercise, and thus to fulfill, in the highest degree, the purposes for which it was designed.

— *Cavendish on whist, about 1860*

38

CLIENTS

It's hustling, exactly like prostitution, at least in one way.
— Garey Hayden

In a way, my job is to keep the client's hand off the cards, not let him make a mistake.
— Garey Hayden

Pros can't do everything.
— Garey Hayden, commenting on a 97 game on a 156 average

Well then, they should abolish lessons in all forms of everything.
— Paul Soloway's response to a critical question about "pay for play"

I'm not sure whether glory or masterpoints is first on the list, but I know learning to play better is definitely last.
— Eddie Kantar on the motivation of clients

It is difficult to classify the type of persons who will engage the services of a bridge professional. They run the gamut of those whose only intent is to learn the finer points of the game, through people who are already reasonably proficient but are anxious to play only with the very best, and are unable to get a partner in that category without paying for the privilege. Finally, a fairly large group consists of those incompetent as players, possibly elderly and disgruntled or irritable and not particularly reasonable, who do not have many bridge player friends or acquaintances, and find it almost impossible to get any kind of partner. These unfortunates will hire a pro primarily to have someone to play with, someone with whom they will occasionally finish "in the money," and only as a secondary reason to improve their game.
— Ivan Erdos

Famous BRIDGE Players

Dwight Eisenhower: Eisenhower maintained a keen interest in bridge throughout his military and political careers, and even into retirement. Described by Oswald Jacoby as a "superior" player, Eisenhower used bridge as a frequent form of recreation while Supreme Allied Commander before the invasion of Normandy, while NATO chief in Paris, and in the White House. When asked who he would choose as his NATO deputy in 1950 he answered, "Al Gruenther — he's the best bridge player."

George Burns: Burns is an avid rubber bridge player, often spending many hours a day at the table with Hollywood friends. That could be one of the things keeping him mentally fit in his 90's. As he put it in an interview in 1982, "I think people can't help getting older, but you don't have to get 'old.' Nobody has to get old. You know, if you practice getting old long enough, you'll eventually be a success. None of that. That's silly. Getting old. You take little steps, you don't get there. Anyway, I'm making old age fashionable. People can't wait to get old now." P.S. I wonder if "God" ever makes a mistake at the bridge table.

Omar Sharif: In addition to being a world famous actor, Sharif has represented Egypt in world bridge competition, and once remarked that he valued the smallest bridge trophy more than any of his acting awards. Since 1975 Sharif has been credited as co-author of Goren's syndicated bridge column. Sharif is still active in European bridge tournaments.

I do not particularly enjoy the game when playing with the average client. The bridge field is in many ways just like any other business. Ask someone selling merchandise in a store, soliciting insurance, or doing clerical work, whether they enjoy their activities. Most likely they will tell you that they do it out of economic necessity. I have always considered myself very lucky because I am getting paid for doing something I can well tolerate and sometimes even enjoy. There are times when playing professionally with incompetent, difficult and neurotic people becomes quite a chore. But there are many tournaments I enjoy immensely, and many clients who have become close personal friends . . . for this I am indeed grateful.

— *Ivan Erdos*

COFFEEHOUSING

Madam, that second hesitation was certainly an overbid.
— Charles Goren

I'd like a review of the bidding with all the original inflections.
— George S. Kaufman

Which half of your singleton club do you intend to play?
*— Player with perfect count on the hand
to fumbling RHO*

COMPETITION

The first step toward winning at bridge is to become not only suspicious and watchful of others but also to realize that for the most part, you are playing with a group of people who have the instincts of ax murderers.
— Jerry Sohl

Playing international matchpoints is more exhausting than pro football. It's brutal and the pressures far exceed those of any other sport.
— Ira Corn

It is brutal, more brutal than football. In bridge you have laid your full ego and psychological self on the table against your opponents.
— Ira Corn

It's like four people boxing at the same time.
— Robert Bonomi, ACBL public relations

Feminists should take note that there are no queens in Italian, Spanish or German playing cards; instead, each suit has two knights (jacks). It was the romantic French who replaced one knight with a queen, and queens remain on our cards to this day.

In comparison to bridge, hockey is for pantywaists. Compared to the effects of trumping your partner's ace, football is for sissies. Bridge players are mean, sarcastic and gleeful in victory. Who else would refer to having won one hand as 'having a leg on' and being 'vulnerable' unless they were the kind of people who would kick the crutches away from a cripple.
> — *Catherine Ford, Canadian newspaper writer*

The thing I was most proud of was that I set out to beat the record of football's Walter Payton, who had 2,003 yards in one season. I beat him by six yards. I had 2,009, but he played a shorter season.
> — *Ron Andersen, on setting a new McKenney record in 1977*

The minority of people — I like to call them the elite — prefer to compete with their brains rather than competing physically. These are the bridge players.
> — *Easley Blackwood*

The people who still play (bridge) are the people who thrive on mental challenges. Today most people seem more interested in being spectators than being participants. So much entertainment is passive.
> — *Max Hardy*

In what other activity could the extraordinary feat of the late Oswald Jacoby be repeated?
> — *Joyce Nicholson*

An unbelievable man . . . a dying man in his eighties, totally concentrated through grueling 30-board and 32-board sessions of board-a-match, fighting every bit as fiercely as always, playing magnificently and enjoying it.
> — *"The Bridge World" on Oswald Jacoby winning the Reisinger in Miami, 1983*

He likes to mentally crush the opponents.
> — *Bobby Wolff on Bob Hamman*

I like the moment when I break a man's ego.

As social and genteel as contract bridge is portrayed to the public eye, the truth is that the game resembles war. This is why people love it so much. It allows us to fulfill our darker competitive desires without really hurting our fellow human being. Even in the afternoon duplicate, blood is spilled on every trick; on every hand a battle is won or lost.

— *Matthew Granovetter*

COMPLAINING

Usually the fellow who complains most about his partner is a grade-A bridge criminal in his own right. Call it a Freudian defense mechanism, or a guilt complex, or an exploitation of the military theory that the best defense is a good attack — whatever your explanation you will find that the fellow who is more vehement during the post-mortem has almost invariably been chiefly at fault in the catastrophe that has just been perpetrated in the name of bridge.

— *Sam Fry, Jr.*

All-Funeral BRIDGE Team
1. Alan BELL
2. George COFFIN
3. Allan GRAVES
4. Harold LILIE
5. Bobby NAIL
6. George REITH
7. Tobias STONE
8. William GRIEVE
9. Betty VAIL

COMPLEXITY

Many people think chess is complicated. Chess is a simple game in comparison to bridge.

— Robert Bonomi

COMPUTER BRIDGE

Everyone reckons that bridge is a mathematical game — but only five percent is down to cold, scientific calculations. The rest are human factors — psychology, imagination and self-preparation for the adventure that's about to happen. Now, all computers can only do things that are pre-programmed. They can never react to the moment, and that is what human beings are best at.

— Zia Mahmood

COMPUTER HANDS

Paranoia is a disease of tournament bridge players. They feel themselves to be the victims of modern technology — the computer is out to get them.

— Alan Truscott

CONVENTIONS

Bidding has become very scientific. Primitive methods will no longer suffice.

— Peter Weichsel

It is only the cripple that must depend on crutches.

— Rixi Markus

The more often I encounter complicated artificial systems, the more strongly I feel about their futility.

— Rixi Markus

BRIDGE-Playing Cities (Population)

1. Bridgewater, England 26,800
2. Bridgend, Wales 15,260
3. Bridge of Allan, Scotland 4,285
4. Bridgetown, Australia 1,569
5. Bridgetown, Barbados 12,430
6. Bridgeport, CT 388,953
7. Bridge, ID 140
8. Bridgehampton, NY 900
9. Bridge City, TX 8,164
10. Bridgeland, VT 150

Conflicting conventions have changed what was once the basis for a nice, friendly evening into an inferno of disagreement.

— "The Saturday Evening Post," 1930

A precious lot of good they are if your partner doesn't understand them. I consider them poisonous devices and would abolish the lot.

— Unknown

They are a substitute for thinking — the opium of the masses, as Lenin used to say. We all know that the rapport one has with a favorite partner is worth all the conventions in the books, while no convention will save you when you have as partner your favorite opponent.

— Mollo's Hideous Hog

I cannot believe that ordinary human beings will want to play a game which requires the constant use of a code book.

*— Ewart Kempson, editor of the
"Bridge Magazine," 1960*

In spite of their artificial systems, the New Zealand pairs make many natural bids — about four or five each session.

If I went to one of my clubs for a rubber of bridge, and found that one of my opponents was using a highly artificial system of bidding, I would quit. That sort of thing is not a recreation, but merely a boring waste of time. And I'm quite sure that if it is allowed it will eventually result in the death of the game.

Are your ruling bodies so incapable of seeing the wood for the trees that they lay down requirements in terms of points for a natural call yet allow such nauseating paraphernalia as Stayman responses, transfer bids, Sputnik doubles, and worst of all, psychic controls? It is entirely contrary to the spirit of the game that a player should enjoy the advantages of a bluff bid with almost none of the risks. The one convention we need now is a Geneva Convention to protect players from that and all other forms of poison gas. While just a few bids are left that mean what they say, will you use your influence to eliminate from the game all suit bids that are cyphers bearing no relation to the suit named?

As the laws are shortly to be revised, one can only hope that the law-givers will see the light; for just as a multiplicity of conventions killed whist, so the modern multiplicity of conventions is killing contract. It would be a pity to see it crash to death by convention being piled on convention until the whole top-heavy structure falls with a sickening thud . . .

The most dangerous of the lot! Blackwood is much too simple and too addictive. Anyone can get hold of it and swallow an overdose. It's responsible for more fatalities than any other drug on the convention card.

— The Hideous Hog on Blackwood

Of course, there is no such thing as patenting a bid and collecting a royalty on it, but if Blackwood had a nickel for every time his bid was properly used he'd be a rich man, indeed; if he had a nickel for every time it was misused, he'd be a multimillionaire.

— Richard Frey

Once somebody called me the Simple Simon of bridge. I said, "Thank you very much. I appreciate the compliment."

— Charles Goren

The proliferation of devious and intricate bidding conventions is a source of alarm to the majority of bridge players who like their bridge games pleasant and uncomplicated.

— Florence Osborn, 1964

	Age if still living Jan.1,1990	Year of death
Here is a list of 7 famous names in the history of whist and bridge, and how old they would be if still living (plus year of death):		
1. Edmond Hoyle (of "According to Hoyle" fame, English, first recognized authority on bridge and other card games)	310	1769
2. Alexandre Louis Honore Lebreton Deschapelles (of "Deschapelles Coup" fame, French whist authority, considered the world's best in his day)	209	1847
3. Cavendish (pseudonym of Henry Jones, famous London whist authority who had New York City's Cavendish Club named after him)	158	1899
4. John Mitchell (father of duplicate whist, developed pairs movement still used today in bridge tournaments, wrote first book on tournament organization)	135	1914
5. Milton C. Work (the Charles Goren of whist and auction bridge, author of the point-count system)	125	1934
6. Wilbur C. Whitehead (an early bridge authority, one of the first successful bridge authors)	123	1931
7. Ralph C. Richards (founder and president of the ACBL)	113	1943

I know players who have a closetful of conventions and a head full of swirling confusions and a genuine need to see a psychiatrist.
— *Charles Goren*

The complex Simons of Bridge, the players who rush from convention to convention and system to system, give me a pain, not merely because they are slowing down their own progress to genuine bridge skill but because they make life so unpleasant for everybody else.
— *Charles Goren*

How far players should be permitted to go in the use of artificial bids is a question that has been agitating tournament circles for some time now.
— *Albert Ostrow in 1955*

Conventions will eventually kill bridge as a recreation. Over-emphasis of the bidding conventions caused the downfall of whist. Over-emphasis of the bidding conventions will do the same to contract birdge. (Artificial bids) are . . . an attempt to take away, by confusion, the legal values dealt to players by the fall of the cards.
— *Letter to the Bulletin of the American Contract Bridge League, many decades ago*

The player who arrives at a tournament with a long list of artificial conventions is spending too much time trying to win instead of trying to have fun. The irony is he'll wind up doing neither. This sort of player is a burden to himself, his partner, and his opponents.
— *Charles Goren*

Another reason for dropouts (from duplicate bridge) is the proliferation of conventions. The average player comes to a game to have a good time, not to read through a lot of fine print.
— *Ernest Rovere*

Ely (Culbertson) gave bridge an international language. Americans and Japanese, French, English, Germans, Italians all found in bridge a common tongue and a common bond. What has happened to this great game today? At the top, the universal language has been lost in a tower of Babel. The common bond has been dissolved in a plethora of systems and signals, cryptograms and codes, punctuated by alerts, protests and appeals.

— Victor Mollo

The use of conventions isn't a skill; more often than not, it's an obstacle to skill's development. You'll find that conventions have a nasty habit of creeping unobtrusively into your system . . .

— Peter Donovan

Tournament bridge has created a new breed of player, who has become "gadget" crazy . . . the true gadgeteer will want to give an artificial meaning to as many bids as possible. The balance of artificiality far outweighs the element of naturality about the system, so perhaps it's time to have a government health warning printed on convention cards: "Artificiality can damage your game!"

— Peter Donovan

It has been said . . . that every time a new convention is introduced, 10,000 bridge players walk out the door.

— Marcus Wood, Sr.

Faced with a tough hand, every bridge player wants to know what the world's top players would bid — but not if their bidding is incomprehensible.

— Omar Sharif

The road to hell is paved with good conventions.

— Anonymous

Obscure BRIDGE Term Quiz

11. Dormitzer: a. a place where many kibitzers can be found; b. a kibitzer of low intelligence; c. a tray on which refreshments are served during a bridge game; d. analysis of play by a kibitzer. Answer on page 109.

COUNTING

The chances are that if you asked an average seven-year-old to add five and four and one and subtract the total from 13 he would come up with the right answer. Why is it then, that so many intelligent adults produce the wrong one at the card table?

— *Victor Mollo*

DECEPTIVE PLAY

You can always trust a rattlesnake, so long as you can think as he does.

— *The Hideous Hog*

Most bridge players are larcenous at heart. The better an expert plays, the more larceny lies under his vest.

— *Alfred Sheinwold*

DEFENSE

The average defender operates in a fog of uncertainty.

— *H. W. Kelsey*

Anyone can become a decent bidder. Most people can become decent declarers. When a person defends well, that person is deemed "a bridge player."

— *Matthew Granovetter*

If defense is the toughest part of the game to master, as most writers maintain, then the opening lead must be the single most difficult aspect of the game.

— *Frank Stewart*

Regardless of what sadistic impulses we may harbor, winning bridge means helping partner avoid mistakes.

— *Frank Stewart*

What makes the difference between the average strong player and the superstar at bridge? I suggest that the answer lies partly in defensive ability. The world is full of competent declarers, but the truly expert defender is a rare bird indeed.

— Hugh Kelsey

In my opinion, an airtight defensive game is the most valuable asset a contract player can have.

— P. Hal Sims

A player who can't defend accurately should try to be declarer.

— Alfred Sheinwold

EGO

Do not be overly impressed by the player who boasts he has been playing for 25 years. After all, 25 years' experience may be no more than one year's experience repeated 24 times.

— Ron Klinger

Every human being who ever sat down at a bridge table thinks he is a better player than he actually is. There are no exceptions to this; none.

— Ely Culbertson

The Men-of-the-Cloth BRIDGE Team

1. E. Farrington ABBOTT
2. Cliff BISHOP
3. Eddie KANTAR
4. Charles MONK
5. David PRIEST
6. Norman SQUIRE

It's a fact of life in bridge that most players think they're better than they are.

— *Alan Sontag*

I next concentrated on the improvement of my bridge game. I wanted to become the "greatest player on earth."

— *Ely Culbertson, "The Strange Lives of One Man, An Autobiography"*

In dealing with publicity, I also kept in mind three basic appeals, to the ego, to fear, and to sex. The mass mind remembers best by tying up events with its own emotional experience; and everywhere, the individual seeks to project and to identify his own personality. Bridge would have to be dramatized and made intellectually significant so as to appeal to the ego.

— *Ely Culbertson*

Reporter: Mr. Culbertson, in your opinion, who is the best player in the world?
Culbertson: Me.
Reporter: And the second-best player?
Culbertson: Me, too.
Reporter: And the third?
Culbertson: Me. You see, I am all three — the first, second and third best player in the world. After that comes a gulf and then all the other players.

— *Culbertson in response to a reporter's questions*

Your challenge is accepted with pleasure. All these years I have been itching to lay my bridge hands on you. At last you have emerged from your hiding place to meet your master. Though I consider you one of the world's finest card players even your brilliancy cannot overcome the handicaps of your atrocious system.

— *Culbertson accepting, in writing, Hal Sims' challenge to a bridge match*

Another John Crawford, of course.

— John Crawford, upon being asked, who
would be the ideal partner

ETHICS

It is a good deal easier to play irreproachably than to play well.

— Victor Mollo

One should always play fairly when one has the winning cards.

— Oscar Wilde

The History of BRIDGE

Have you ever wondered how the modern game of bridge got started? It developed in four basic stages — whist, bridge whist, auction bridge and contract bridge.

Whist: Like modern contract bridge, whist, a game of 16th century English origin, is played by four people, two partnerships. Fifty-two cards are dealt, 13 to each player. The last card is turned face up on the table and becomes the trump suit. The card remains on the table until it is the dealer's turn to play to the first trick, when he may return it to his hand.

The player to the dealer's left makes the opening lead, and play proceeds as in bridge except that all four hands are concealed. There is no dummy.

Six tricks are book. Eack trick, in excess of six counts one point. In other words, there is no bidding. Chance determines the trump suit on each hand.

Rubber bonuses and honor bonuses are provided for.

Bridge Whist: Bridge whist succeeded whist in popularity until auction bridge took over in the 20th century.

The trump suit is no longer determined by turning over the last card dealt. Instead, the dealer or his partner is allowed to name the trump suit or to choose notrump (notrump play didn't exist at basic whist).

In whist, each trick in excess of book counts one point regardless of which suit is trumps. In bridge whist, the four suits and notrump have varying values but, strangely enough, spades are at the bottom of the ladder, followed by clubs, diamonds, hearts (the highest ranked suit) and notrump.

It is also possible for the opponents to double, and the dealer's side to redouble and so on, indefinitely, thus introducing a strong "gambling" feature to the game.

There is still no bidding but dealer's partner's hand is exposed during play, thus introducing the dummy.

(Continued on Page 73)

EXCUSES
(RESPONSES TO THE INQUIRY,
"HOW WAS YOUR GAME?")

We just had a few partnership misunderstandings, that's all.

> Translation: We had a bad game.

There were ups and downs.

> Translation: There were more downs than ups. We had a bad game.

Can't tell for sure. Probably somewhere around average, maybe a little below.

> Translation: Way below. We had a bad game.

We sat the wrong direction.

> Translation: We had a bad game.

We didn't get any cards.

> Translation: We had a bad game.

We could have done without a couple of boards.

The hands weren't very interesting.

We just followed suit.

I don't think we'll wait around for the scores.

Mind your own business.

> Translation: We had a bad game.

Universal Laws of BRIDGE

- As soon as you notice you are having a good game, something bad will happen.
- No matter how many problems you anticipate on a hand, something you hadn't anticipated will come up.
- As soon as a tough problem arises on a hand that you really have to think about, the director will call, "All move for the next round please" and break your concentration.
- Whenever you think you have pulled all the trumps, someone still has one left.

EXPERTS

Bridge experts are a weird and motley group.

— Jack Olsen

One of the greatest conspiracies of modern times is the pretense that contract bridge can be played and that anybody ever actually does so. The fact is, of course, that no more than five people ever played the game; and four of them are known to be incurable liars.

— Alfred Sheinwold

Whether they reach more good contracts than did their predecessors is debatable. That they have more disasters on the way is certain. All the masters have technique at their fingertips, but it doesn't stop them from committing atrocities.

— Victor Mollo

So many lawsuits have been brought against me by aggrieved authorities and rivals that I actually learned law while defending them. In the "Bridge World Magazine," I once called a bridge authority an "average player." He sued me for $100,000 for libel! He's *still* an average player.

— Ely Culbertson

BRIDGE Trivia Quiz

12. Which is more likely: a hand with nine high card points or a hand with 11 high card points? Answer on page 109.
13. What is the Rabbi's Rule? Answer on page 111.
14. To what playing card did Charlie Brown in "Peanuts" once compare himself? Answer on page 111.
15. What is the most points you can lose on a single bridge hand? Answer on page 111.

When you give an expert a bad score in a tournament, he may compliment you on your play, but he really wants to bend the duplicate board over your head.

— *Unknown*

Do not look for a book to help you become an expert. There are books that will take you from beginner to advanced intermediate, but the final transition to expertdom comes about from playing, talking, and living bridge with other monomaniacs during every waking hour of many months, sometimes many years. This is not written in scorn; supremacy in *any* field is the product of talent applied to the point of monomania.

— *Alfred Sheinwold*

If it is true that the borderline between genius and insanity is very narrow, then it is equally true that the difference between "brilliant" and "crazy" play at bridge is very much a matter of opinion and point of view.

— *Sidney Lenz*

The pleasure at expert level comes in equal measure from a heightened awareness of the intricate structure of cards, from the ability in one sphere of activity to produce order out of chaos, and from an occasional glimpse of metaphysical delights that are normally hidden from the eyes of men.

— *Hugh Kelsey*

A bridge expert can be described in simple terms as a player who makes fewer mistakes than most.

— *Hugh Kelsey*

The real secret of the expert is to make logic seem like flair.

— *Hugh Kelsey*

The experts may play better bridge but everyone else may have more fun.

— *Robert Bonomi*

HANDHOGS

Perhaps you have noticed a strange phenomena about poor bridge players. The worse they play the cards the more they seem to grab the contract.

— Howard Schenken

Bridge is a 52-card game. This simple statement is overlooked by many bridge players. All too often the bridge player thinks of the game as a 13-card game — the hand he holds.

— Ira Corn

But there is one player whom I have never learned how to cope with and that is the player who never stops to consider that you also hold 13 cards; he will ignore your bids, he will pay no attention to your warnings, come hell or high water he will take command of the hand, and when he has been doubled and gone down several tricks, he'll ascribe it to nothing but bad luck. You are fortunate if he doesn't smile blandly and say, "Well, I think it was worth it, partner." I am still looking for the book that will show me how to deal with him. Shooting is too quick and too painless, and besides, there might not be another fourth available.

— Somerset Maugham

Please, please partner, let me play the hand. I assure you that it's in your own interest.

— The Hideous Hog

INDIVIDUAL (EVENT)

Trial by ordeal.

— Anonymous

Never again.

— Anonymous

INTERNATIONAL BRIDGE

If they played bridge they wouldn't have so much time to hate each other.

— *Omar Sharif asked about the
Middle East situation*

IMPS VS. MATCHPOINTS
(THE DIFFERENCE)

Who do you think were the two best heavyweights who ever fought? I don't really care who you pick, but take those two fighters, both at the peak of their careers, put them in a ring and let them slug it out for 15 rounds. Whoever wins is the champ. That's IMPs. Now take the same two fighters, blindfold them and tie one hand behind their backs. Divide the ring diagonally with a solid barrier and put a heavyweight on each side of the barrier. Now go down to the local tavern and collect 20 drunks. Place 10 drunks on each side of the ring and let the fighters go at it. Whoever knocks out his drunks first is the winner. That's matchpoints!"

— *Bob Hamman*

HISTORY (OF BRIDGE)

Take this simple game (whist), add a dummy, the concept of notrump, bidding, and an occasional felonious assault, and you have contract bridge.

— *Jack Olsen*

The name "duplicate" as used in bridge was derived from a combination of the words "dupe" and "locate." In the game of duplicate, the purpose is literally "locate the dupes" or show up the dumb bunnies in the crowd.

— *Joe James*

It's just a fad.
Auction is good enough for us.
Contract will die in a few months.
— *Comments by expert players at New York's
Knickerbocker Whist Club in 1927*

The great cartoonist, H. T. Webster, had as good a theory as any of the murky ancestry of bridge. In a 1930 drawing in the New York *World,* he pictured two devils sitting at a card table in the acrid smokes of hell. One is explaining, "It's a game for four. Everyone has to bid and I've thrown in a lot of conventions to make it more confusing. I call it bridge, and if it doesn't get results I've got another variation that's surefire. This will be known as contract, and I'll bet my pitchfork, it will demoralize the human race."

— *Jack Olsen*

In England, whips often had difficulty holding quorums in the House of Parliament; the honorable members would be off in the anterooms playing auction.

— *Jack Olsen*

As a matter of legal history, the courts were called on to take cognizance of a number of bridge offenses. One important case came before the Liverpool Police Court, where the accused was charged with a serious assault on his partner. Counsel for the defense, while admitting a technical offense, pleaded extenuating circumstances. The Bench, in applying the Probation Act, clearly accepted that the defendant had been subjected to the grossest provocation when it appeared that the complainant had opened the bidding two clubs on the exiguous holding of king, queen, and two small ones. Indeed, one feels that the wrong man was in the dock.

— *Rex Mackey*

KIBITZERS

Card players consider the kibitzer the lowest form of animal life.

— *Albert Ostrow*

Kibitzers should be paid the proper rate for the job. Nobody should be expected to watch man's inhumanity to man at his own expense.

— *Victor Mollo*

A distinctive feature of bridge is that it's a game to play, not to watch others play.

— *Victor Mollo*

What is the most intractable problem at bridge? As any expert will tell you, it is, without a doubt, the kibitzer evil. He holds power without responsibility and can plague all the players all the time, sitting back happily in the knowledge that no one can hit back.

— *Victor Mollo*

There is the classic story . . . about the faultless kibitzer who watched with keen interest for six hours and never opened his mouth. At this point a bitter argument arose among the players, and finally they agreed to leave the decision to the kibitzer. He shook his head sadly. "Sorry," he said, "I don't know the game."

— *Lee Hazen*

LEARNING BRIDGE

I started playing when I was 16. It kind of interfered with my college education. I went for six years, but never graduated.

— *Alan Sontag*

60

LIFE MASTERS

Their phenomenal memories enable them to recall every successful hand they ever played. Their recollection of disastrous sets is not quite so acute.

— *James Kilpatrick*

LUCK

No matter who writes the books or articles, South holds the most terrific cards I ever saw. There is a lucky fellow if I ever saw one.

— *George S. Kaufman*

Luck is where preparation meets opportunity.

— *Anonymous*

It was simple. I just used the Moe Convention. I just went eeney, meeney, miney, moe, and finessed 'moe' for the queen of spades.

— *Bridge player explaining how she located the queen of trumps in a slam*

You play the hand that's been dealt you. There may be pain in that hand or there may not be pain in that hand, but you play the hand that's dealt you.

— *Jim Brady, press secretary to Ronald Reagan, shot by John Hinckley, Jr.*

Obscure BRIDGE Term Quiz

16. Elder: a. the oldest player at the table; b. the most experienced player in the game; c. opening leader; d. player who plays last to the first trick, i.e., declarer.
17. Gulpic: a. slang for a shaded opening bid; b. slang for an egreglously bad bid; c. to cause partner anxiety while you're playing the hand; d. a deep finesse. Answers on page 111.

MARRIED BRIDGE PLAYERS

Husbands and wives make poor partners — unless they happen to be someone else's husband or wife.

— Milton Ozaki

The most volatile bridge partnerships are husbands and wives.

— Catherine Ford

If your spouse is a dedicated bridge player, and if you want your marriage to endure, play with someone else.

— Milton Ozaki

Since bridge is essentially an ego game, unless both partners are mentally tough, one or the other will dominate.

— Mary Baptist

We believe that the bridge table is used as a socially acceptable place to get rid of frustrations in a marriage.

— Jim and Lois Scott

If you play bridge with your wife as partner, you need at least 20 points to open, and it wouldn't hurt to have 25.

— Joe James

As for domestic discord, bridge never broke up a home that was not ripe for disruption anyway.

— Elmer Davis

Opposing bridge systems are not grounds for divorce.

— Judge's ruling several decades ago

World statistics of divorce directly or indirectly attributable to (bridge) are not, of course, readily available, but it may be of interest to the social researcher to learn that in January 1935 it was announced in the Divorce Court in Budapest that 54 marriages were dissolved in Hungary the previous year as a result of bridge playing by women.

— Rex Mackey

In sex I made full use of the ever-popular husband and wife angle at the bridge table; their arguments, their quarrels, a few divorces, and even a murder or two. I recommended bigger and better fights at the bridge table, as an escape from the hundreds of petty inhibitions and annoyances accumulated in the course of daily married life.

— Ely Culbertson on publicizing bridge

When married couples play bridge in partnership, they will inadvertently reveal in microcosm, the entire story of their married lives.

— Fleur Tamon, "The Houston Post"

MASTERMINDING

Perhaps good bids are not necessarily good bids when made with a partner who is likely to get confused by them.

— Matthew Granovetter

The best bid in the world isn't worth a thing if partner doesn't know what it means.

— Unknown

MASTERPOINTS

Master Points! Why the whole idea is cockeyed. If you reward success, you should punish failure. If you present Master Points for merit you should inflict Monster Points for demerit. I have nothing against virtue, as such, but why should sin go unpunished? In due course, we'll have Master Monsters and Life Monsters, just as they do with Master Points.

— The Hideous Hog

MISTAKES

Learn from the mistakes of others. You won't live long enough to make them all yourself.

— *Alfred Sheinwold*

A "mistake" in bridge is any action, either in the bidding or the play, which I, in similar circumstances, would not take.

— *Edgar Kaplan*

Even the very best players can produce a flawless session only rarely. Where the novice might make between 50 and 100 mistakes a session (not all those mistakes cost, thank heavens), the expert would make less than half a dozen.

— *Ron Klinger*

Bridge without error is a goal to which we all aspire. In fact, it is only a fantasy.

— *Ron Klinger*

Tournament bridge players . . . average from 10 to 25 major sins per session depending on how well they get along with their idiot partners and how well they stand up under pressure.

— *Marshall Smith*

In bridge, opportunity knocks at every second deal and failure to grab it by the hair accounts for the invisible leak through which all the profits flow out.

— *Ely Culbertson*

As so many bridge writers have pointed out, bridge is a game of mistakes. If you make fewer mistakes than your opponents, you are bound to be a consistent winner.

— *Richard Nagel*

I have made a mistake. The second mistake in less than six years. People will be saying that I am losing my touch.

— *The Hideous Hog*

I will point out some of the purely theoretical considerations that influenced me in creating Ely the Celebrity. In formulating this "public personality" I kept in mind two important factors. First, a popular personality must have defects that humanize him. Therefore, I concentrated most of my ingenuity on the glorification of my defects as a personality and as a bridge player. I never failed to feature my glaring errors in bidding and play. In this manner I became widely known not only for my brilliant coups (which, of course, I sedulously publicized) but for my atrocities as well (which gave me more than double the amount of publicity).

— Ely Culbertson in his autobiography

OPENING BIDS

I favor light opening bids. When you're my age, you're never sure they're going to get back to you in time.

— Oswald Jacoby in 1979 at the age of 77

It is well known that in third seat you must have 13 cards to open the bidding.

— Edgar Kaplan

OPENING LEADS

Opening leads are a science . . . an art . . . a sheer guess.

— Anonymous

Years ago, there were only two acceptable excuses for not leading the suit your partner had opened; having no cards in the suit, and sudden death.

— Alfred Sheinwold

If I've told you once I've told you three times, don't lead my suit unless I bid it three times.

— Ron Andersen to partner in
1979 Vanderbilt

Discipline is required and discipline means restraining your imagination. It's sad but true: the mundane lead is usually best.

— *Matthew Granovetter*

OPPONENTS

We should all love and cooperate with other human beings, but this principle doesn't apply to our bridge opponents.

— *Alfred Sheinwold*

OVERBIDDING

A man shouldn't oughtta open his mouth, unless he got a hand to back it up.

— *Cowboy on "Gunsmoke"*

The overbidder is the most prevalent (type of card player). His fault, in time, takes on the aspects of drug taking. Indulgence fails to cure him. Many overbidders actually recognize the errors of their way, but they take pride in being known as "bold bidders." They suffer from a showmanship complex from which they never recover.

— *P. Hal Sims*

All-World BRIDGE Team

1. Robert JORDAN
2. Marshall MILES
3. Freddie NORTH
4. Morris PORTUGAL
5. George RHODE
6. Norman BERLIN
7. Robert ISRAEL
8. Pat SPAIN
9. Leslie WEST

Edgar Kaplan (or was it A. J. Moyse?) in the pages of "The Bridge World" pined for the good old days when if one held 21-high card points in fourth seat, he could be sure the bidding to him would be pass, pass, pass. Now the bidding is at the three or four level before you've counted to 20.

— *Robert Sundby, "Bridge in the 80's"*

A fool's mouth is his destruction.

— *Proverbs 18:7*

I figured you were in trouble at three, so you might as well be in trouble at four.

— *Player raising his partner's preempt to game with a void*

Are bidders more aggressive nowadays? Is jack-sixth and out all it takes to preempt?

— *Robert Sundby, "Bridge in the 80's"*

Contract bridge players demonstrate a similar anxiety (or fear) that time is running out. In the auction of a hand, the player feels he must bid a suit at any cost, even vulnerable or risk losing the opportunity. In the same way players of life feel they must enter into every avenue of temptation that comes their way out of fear of missing that one great miracle moment. "Is life passing me by?" their psyche asks. Likewise, the contract player, with little to risk but a poor score, enters the bidding on risky values in the fear of missing that one great miracle trump-fit.

— *a noted 1930's psychiatrist comparing fear of not getting into the auction with fear of death*

Overbidders are generally good card players, often with touches of brilliance in their game. They fulfill a certain number of doubled contracts which should never have been bid in the first place. These triumphs act as a stimulus which bars them from all hopes of cure. They remember their infrequent successes, forgetting completely that each of these Pyrrhic victories was preceded by at least eight poor results and two outright disasters.

— *P. Hal Sims*

OVERHEARD (AT THE BRIDGE TABLE)

Bridge would be a lot better game if only you didn't need a partner.

I think we're all a little masochistic. Otherwise, why would we continue to play bridge?

I need 10 more masterpoints for Life Master, 15 of which must be gold.

My partner played very well today, except he was playing some game other than bridge.

The hand should have been passed out, but with entry fees the way they are today . . .

We had a partnership misunderstanding. My partner assumed I knew what I was doing.

Who wants to take off work for the Men's Pairs? I'd rather go to the zoo.

A card must be played the same day it is dealt.

My partner is 20 years behind the times. Nowadays you pay your money to bid. My partner still thinks you need cards.

I led out of turn to my own contract.

Six notrump, good contract. Cold on three defensive errors.

Well, we didn't win, but at least we weren't humiliated.

Two hearts, making six. A plus is a plus.

If you don't have a heart, play a faded black card.

My partner's a better opening leader than I do.

I bid hearts twice at the three level.

For some strange reason, minus 1700 never seems to get you many matchpoints.

If I hadn't gone down, I would have made it.

I've tried relaxing at the bridge table but I feel more comfortable tense.

Your play was much better tonight, and so were your excuses.

We play forcing hesitations.

Every hand is like the landing of an airplane. If you can walk away from it, it's fine.

An absolute zero is a result that can't possibly be repeated across the field.

I went down in my contract because of bad distribution. Each of my opponents had 13 cards.

You know you're in trouble when the first thing the opponents decide to do is draw trumps — and you're declarer.

If I was in four I would have made five but because I was in five I only made four.

I don't know what my probem is. Either I drink too much while I'm playing bridge or I play too much bridge while I'm drinking.

It was a 50-50 slam. It either makes or it doesn't.

A 20-point hand re-evaluates to zero when the opponents take the setting trick.

A zero is a zero is a zero.

It's an easy hand to make. You just have to guess where everything is.

The field will probably be there.
> — *Remark made after a player and his partner failed to bid a cold game in a Swiss teams event*

Bridge is a game where a mass of people sit down to be frustrated.
> — *A caddie's observation*

The perfect game eludes us.
> — *One player to his partner after totaling up 205 on a 156 average.*

Would you believe that they even had an auction where they managed to bar each other?
> — *A Swiss teams player complaining about his teammates*

Director to young man watching the bridge tournament: "Would you care to kibitz, sir?"
Young man: "No thanks, I'll just watch."

PARTNERS

Rothman was a student of human nature, and began trying to figure out the reasons for the way bridge affected those who played it. The game, he decided had many of the trademarks of a disease. It was rather like malaria with its alternating periods of high fever and relatively normal health. (He assumed that bridge players did have periods of normal health, because it seemed improbable that they could survive if they always ran with such high temperatures.) It was possible also that, as in the case of malaria, there was some kind of carrier like the anopheles mosquito that transmitted the disease from avid bridge players to healthy individuals.

Certain facts, though, did not fit the disease theory. If bridge was a disease, why didn't some lucky victims develop an immunity to it? And why couldn't it be cured by putting the victims in isolation wards, while their cards and bridge books were burned by doctors wearing antiseptic masks and biteproof clothing? To the best of his knowledge, however, no bridge player had ever developed an immunity or had been cured, nor did any of them seek a cure. This did not fit the picture of a disease. Furthermore, where had the virus of bridge been lurking in the ages before making its first appearance? No, bridge in itself could not be a disease. It must be the symptom of one.

After long and careful observation, Rothman decided that bridge was a symptom of that deep-seated human ailment; the urge to blame things on a partner . . .

In the first place, of course, there were no excellent partners. At best, a partner was barely adequate. At worst, the partnership was an ogre or a witch out of folklore, lurking across the table and waiting for a chance to butcher a hand. The in-between partner merely had spells of insanity. The partner could always be blamed for everything that went wrong. And fortunately, unlike the marriage partner, the bridge partner could easily be replaced if the need arose.

— Richard Powell, "Tickets to the Devil"

According to an evening paper, there are only five real authorities on bridge in this country. Odd how often one gets one of them as a partner.

— "Punch" (British magazine)

Admittedly the supply of poor partners greatly exceeds the demand.

— Victor Mollo

A fellow had made a bad bid and gone for 1400. "I'm sorry," he said to his partner, "I had a card misplaced." Asked his partner innocently, "Only one card?"

— Charles Goren

Never reproach your partner if there is the slightest thing for which you can reproach yourself.

— Ely Culbertson

On the other hand, do not reproach yourself if you think it would give undue encouragement to your partner's baser instincts.

— Elmer Davis

In chess you're all alone, but it's not as much fun. In other words, I don't enjoy other card games as well. I don't enjoy poker at all. I think because it's me against the world. I enjoy playing *with* somebody. I enjoy doing something *with* someone, and bridge gives me the opportunity.

— Barry Crane

If I did everything right, I wouldn't be playing with you!

— Player to partner after coming under a barrage of criticism for misdefending a hand

You can be the world's greatest bridge player, but some-one else is going to be sitting across the table from you. If you behave in a way — any way, that inhibits that person from playing up to his or her potential, you are not going to get as good a result as you would if you knew how to work with other human beings. It's terribly important.

— *Warren Buffett*

Everybody criticizes their partner. It's natural, but it's not so smart. When you think about it rationally, it must be worth tons of masterpoints to simply keep your mouth shut after partner makes a mistake.

— *Matthew Granovetter*

The minute you scream at partner, you give away something about the hand. The best approach when dummy comes down is to say nothing and concentrate on your play.

— *Matthew Granovetter*

Nothing is more important than partnership confidence.

— *P. Hal Sims*

The History of BRIDGE

Auction Bridge: Auction bridge (the auction principle was introduced in 1904) is the third major step in the evolution of bridge. Bidding is introduced, but the object is to keep the contract as low as possible because declarer's side is credited with the number of tricks won, whether contracted for or not.

If declarer bids two spades and takes 12 tricks, he is credited with making a small slam.

Penalties and premiums in auction are the same without regard to vulnerability but the trick scores change. Provided declarer wins at least the number of tricks over book contracted for, he scores 10, 9, 8, 7 and 6 points for each trick over six in notrump, spades, hearts, diamonds and clubs, respectively. Thirty points constitute a game.

Doubles, redoubles, undertricks and honors are part of the game, as well as slam bonuses. **(Continued on Page 101)**

In contract bridge, the subtle alliance existing between partners is all-important. If the partnership harmony is disrupted, your entire game may collapse.

— *P. Hal Sims*

The full enjoyment of bridge comes from the satisfaction of being able to communicate successfully with your partner. If you can't communicate with partner, you're virtually playing against three people — and you'll never win at this game on your own. Bridge partnerships are rather like marriages — you have to work at them, but the rewards are very worthwhile.

— *Peter Donovan*

Your partner is the most important factor in your bridge development and success.

— *Peter Donovan*

Let me give you a tip. Usually the fellow who complains most about his partner is a grade-A bridge criminal in his own right. Call it a Freudian defense mechanism, or a guilt complex, or an exploitation of the military theory that the best defense is a good attack — whatever your explanation you will find that the fellow who is most vehement during the post-mortem has almost invariably been chiefly at fault in the catastrophe that has just been perpetrated in the name of bridge.

— *Sam Fry, Jr., in an article entitled*
"I Hate Partners"

You bid hearts, he leads spades. You signal a high diamond. He shifts to a club. You make a forcing pass. So does he. What he really wants is an audience, not a partner. His most frequent excuse is "I took a position."

— *Frank Vine on the "One Man Army"*
partner

A man hears what he wants to hear and disregards the rest.

— *Paul Simon*

He doesn't bid, he paints a picture. What never occurs to him is that sooner or later someone has to arrive at a playable contract. That would mean that someone would have to make a decision, and making a decision is one thing he never does. Instead he cuebids and splinters, and forces, and then bids some more, until everyone — partner and opponents — knows every card in his hand, and he is two levels too high. His favorite excuse? "But I had to show you my five-five."

— Frank Vine on the "Vincent Van Gogh" partner

If you had as good a partner as I've got, we'd be in better shape.

— Bridge player, after butchering two auctions in a row, to partner

If life were a bridge game, you'd be a permanent dummy.

— Mr. Dithers to Dagwood

I have always believed that your attitude towards your partner is almost as important as your technical skill at the game.

— Rixi Markus

It is a great and difficult art to play with one's partner. Only a true strategist multiplied by 10 diplomats can manage the motley assortment of humanity facing him. Strategy is as indispensable to the handling of pasteboard freaks as to the handling of human freaks, if one wishes to find himself on the right side of any swing hand.

— Ely Culbertson

One day I may be able to eliminate partner altogether. He will just sit there like a zombie, carrying out my orders, without bidding or playing anything on his own initiative.

— The Hideous Hog

Hell is other people.

— Jean-Paul Sartre

Hell is partner.

— Jean-Paul Sartre if he had been a
bridge player

It's always partner's fault.

— The First Rule of Bridge

PARTNERSHIP DESK

Make it a cute guy and I don't care if he can play bridge.

— Anonymous woman at the partnership desk

PASSING

It is a miracle to me that, in all the literature of bridge, there is not a single chapter on "How to Pass."

— Ely Culbertson

PLAYING FOR BLOOD

It is the man not good enough to win who pleads for the light-hearted approach. His attitude is a pose for his ineptitude. Could he but rub Aladdin's lamp and wish for great ability, there would be no more "only a game" nonsense.

— Norman Squire

BRIDGE Trivia Quiz

18. What is a quack?
19. What card is referred to as the Curse of Scotland?
20. What rule describes the humorous suggestion that an opening lead out of turn should generally be accepted and what is the rationale? Answers on page 111.
21. What color are hippogriffs? Answer on page 112.

PLAY OF THE CARDS

Even if you bid as surely, as confidently, and as brilliantly as a Charlie Goren, Ossie Jacoby, a Don Oakie or a Freddie Sheinwold, all will be for naught if you cannot play the cards.

— Milton Ozaki

More crimes are committed in the play of the trump suit in one session than those recorded in one day in the average city of under 50,000 population.

— Alfred Sheinwold

Unquestionably, the play of the cards (is more difficult than bidding). In 15 days if you wanted to take the trouble, you could become an above-average bidder, but becoming a good card player might take . . . 15 years. But it is a curious thing that the higher the standard of the game, the more important becomes the role of the bidding. Statistics show that in major championships the play of the cards is responsible for at most 25% of the profits and losses. In card play, many champions are close to perfection, while in bidding that is far from true.

— Jose Le Dentu

POST-MORTEM

There are only three aspects to the game — bidding, card play, and defense — though serious players would add another; defending yourself in the post-mortem.

— Paul Burka

There are bridge players who maintain they can't enjoy a game without post-mortems. A certain psychiatrist I know says this is perfectly understandable. These people, he says, need a socially acceptable excuse to blow their tops in public.

— Albert Ostrow

I do not engage in post-mortems, for I think the players who habitually do so make a bore of the most entertaining game that the art of man has devised. The fact is that if you cannot see a mistake when you have made it, no argument will convince you of your error and so the carping critic may just as well hold his peace and deal the next hand.

— *Somerset Maugham*

The worst analysts and the biggest talkers are often one and the same.

— *Frank Stewart*

PRECISION SYSTEM (THE)

With constant practice and studious application, it can be mastered by anyone with an IQ of 460.

— *James J. Kilpatrick*

PROBABILITIES

No bridge book has ever attempted to present a solution to all the situations which may arise. None ever will. There are 635,013,559,600 combinations of the cards.

— *Milton Ozaki*

I figure I average about 15,000 hands of tournament bridge a year. But with a billion possibilities of card combinations per hand, I don't expect to start seeing the same hand until the year 2128.

— *Ron Andersen*

Fascinating in so many other ways, there is one aspect of bridge that bores me intensely — the pursuit of hair-splitting percentages and abstract probabilities.

— *Victor Mollo*

In bridge as in every important sphere in life, horse sense is to mathematics as three is to one. Odds and percentages . . they take the place of thinking, which is why they are so popular.

— *The Hideous Hog*

When I take a fifty-fifty chance, I expect it to come off eight or nine times out of ten.

— *The Hideous Hog*

PROS

Professionalism is the biggest reason for players giving up duplicate. This gnawing cancer finds the average player striving to win the necessary points to become a Life Master by (playing with the pro).

— *Ernest Rovere*

PSYCHERS

His hand will be against every man, and every man's hand is against him.

— *Genesis*

There is no need to psyche against weak opponents. They are quite capable of getting into trouble without assistance.

— *Richard Lederer*

A psychic bid is when you call a suit you haven't got in order to deceive your opponents into thinking you've got what, until you called, they were under the impression they had themselves.

— *Anonymous*

PSYCHOLOGY

Proficiency in bridge depends as much on psychology as it does upon skill.

— *Richard Frey*

Figuring the players is as important as figuring the cards.

— *Easley Blackwood*

Nobody ever went broke underestimating the ability of his opponents.

— *Alfred Sheinwold*

At the bridge table you owe it to your partner to look pleasant; it's dangerous to let the opponents know when you're in trouble.

— *Alfred Sheinwold*

To play well you must know the ropes — including the kind you give an opponent so that he can hang himself.

— *Alfred Sheinwold*

Even the best opponents should be given the chance to err.

— *Victor Mollo*

The second best should be led into temptation at every turn.

— *Victor Mollo*

Because it is a purely intellectual game, it can lift its players to heights of great satisfaction or completely shatter their egos. A good play can salvage an entire day. When you goof, you are crushed. It is a shattering experience.

— *Ira Corn*

Bridge mirrors every facet of life.

— *Victor Mollo*

Bridge is a faithful mirror of life . . . and reflected in the glass you will see the follies and foibles of man shorn of the veils which so carefully hide his ego away from the card table.

— *Victor Mollo*

The true significance of bridge is that it faithfully mirrors life itself. The strong reap the reward of their strength. The weak are justly punished for their weakness.

— *Victor Mollo*

As he bids and plays, his ego comes through to reveal the true man, for at bridge no artist can fail to betray his true nature.

— *Victor Mollo*

There are times when the character of a person can be revealed over a game.

— *Frank Stewart*

You can always judge a man's character by the way he plays cards.

— *Ely Culbertson*

Let nobody think that science has been baffled by contract bridge. The other day, a well-known psychiatrist declared that it was inaccurate to call bridge players crazy. "Insanity is relative," he stated, "and there are hundreds of people who are more insane than bridge players. Well anyway, at least twenty."

— *Albert Ostrow*

But then bridge is much more than a game. An intellectual exercise and at the same time an outlet for the emotions, it mirrors life itself, allowing every player on every deal to express his personality, to be victor and vanquished, plotter and planner, by turns, without ever knowing as he picks up his cards which role he will be called upon to play or how his adventures will end.

— *Victor Mollo*

All-Occupation BRIDGE Team

1. Geoffrey BUTLER
2. Dorothy Jane COOK
3. Jim GARDNER
4. Jim HOOKER
5. Thomas BUTCHER
6. Richard SHEPHERD
7. Bruce PARENT
8. Billy SEAMON
9. Phil WARDEN
10. Carol MINER

There is a delicious but painful form of masochism that has never been recorded in books about abnormal psychology or aberrant sex. It is known as duplicate bridge. It is euphemistically called a 'game,' but it is about as playful as skydiving or shooting the Colorado rapids in a leaky canoe. It is definitely not for the thin-skinned naif with tender sensibilities, high blood pressure or a history of coronary disease. In this game, there are no brownie points awarded for sweet dispositions or good citizenship. This is a competition where the normal elements of generosity, gracious manners and genteel sportsmanship are all laid aside. All that counts is how you score.

— *Fleur Tamon, "The Houston Post"*

One of the popular gathering places for this ritual blood-bath is the (local bridge studio). The open daily member-ship games draw an average of 80-100 people. The players ages range from 19-90, and together they com-prise a veritable human zoo of two-legged loonies.

— *Fleur Tamon*

Want to learn bridge or take on the pros? Or does deflating your ego, suffering humiliation and making yourself out as one of the more brainless living things let loose on this earth sound like a good time? All is possible (at the bridge table).

— Fleur Tamon

If you have the slightest touch of masochism, you'll love this game.

— Player to kibitzer who explained that she didn't know how to play bridge but wanted to learn

Within any flock of chickens there exists a social system that biologists call a peck order. Chicken A has the right to peck all other chickens in the flock. Chicken B has the right to peck all but chicken A, and so on down the line. In tournament bridge the peck order is called masterpoints.

— Richard Powell

It's hard to defend against an inspired declarer.

— Victor Mollo

Behavior such as the high incidence of criticism of self, partner, and opponents, appears to be inconsistent with the idea of enjoyment.

— Jack Stephens, "A Functional Analysis of the Duplicate Bridge Group"

Universal Laws of BRIDGE

- Whomever you play for the queen of trumps doesn't have it.
- If you lead a singleton, partner doesn't have the ace. If you lead something else, he has it.
- The opponents' suit never splits 4-4 when you are in three notrump.

What fascination causes the chronic loser to remain active in the group when there is no reward in the form of group respect or in the form of "ego boost" one gets from victory?

— Jack Stephens

Are such emotional states as anger and disgust, which are frequently displayed at the meetings of the duplicate bridge club, compatible with the concept of "amusement" involved in recreational activities?

— Jack Stephens

Why these games? The play's the thing. Nothing reveals humanity so much as the games they play.

— The Q, alien entity on "Star Trek, the Next Generation"

How we respond to a game tells you more about us than real life.

— Captain Jean-Luc Picard, "Star Trek, the Next Generation"

It is not my intention to make sense of the relationship between the game itself and the aberrant behavior of the monomaniacs who play it at the highest level. Bridge and insanity are certainly intertwined — not only for top-ranked masters but also for dedicated amateurs. I know from my own experience. I devoted a few years to the game and discovered that long before you reach master strength you lose interest in virtually everything that happens away from the bridge table.

— Paul Hoffman in "The Smithsonian" (substitute "chess" for "bridge" and "chessboard" for "bridge table" and you have the original quote)

Remember this — it is never too late to start studying players as well as plays.

— P. Hal Sims

It is the human element in bridge. It is the fact that you are always trying to measure intangibles — the talents and temperaments of three other players. You are always trying to outwit somebody.

— Easley Blackwood

You have got to play the people as well as the cards.

— Easley Blackwood

Figure the people first, then figure the cards.

— Mr. Masters (an Easley Blackwood character)

The play of bridge will allow certain circumstances to arise that are the exact archetypes of what happens in our relationships with people and life in general.

— Lee Lozowick

The evolution and the spiritual development of the human race is right there sitting around the card table . . .

— Lee Lozowick

People literally feel responsible for the cards in their hand as if because they were blindly dealt two points, it is a personal defeat. And not only as if that were a personal defeat but as if God or somebody actually planned such a failure just for them, as if it were somehow intentionally created. You will be truly amazed at how guilty or helpless you feel when you think you are letting down your partner when you can't support his or her bid. You will see people shrug their shoulders and look desperate with a pleading whine of "sorry, partner" on their lips because of a poor hand though it is simply the impersonal way the cards happened to fall.

— Lee Lozowick

Our whole self-image is obvious when we play the game of bridge. If you watch yourself play cards for two rubbers, your whole self-image will be as clear as if somebody had given you a thorough psychological examination. Just watch the way you pick your cards up, the way you sort them, the way you hold them, the way you respond to them, the way you pick up tricks won and the way you throw down cards that you know will not win. The entire spectrum of social and antisocial reactions are enclosed in just a few rubbers of bridge. You can see more about a person in playing bridge for an evening or afternoon than you are normally likely to see in months of social interaction or even in an intimate friendship. This is because in conventional . . . relationships, the participants are always utilizing one of their many masks . . . they are always guarded, always putting their "best foot forward." But in bridge, a harmless game, the guards come down, and the devils lurking within are bared to the world, for all to see.

— *Lee Lozowick*

Famous BRIDGE Players

Winston Churchill: The British war leader and historian played bridge in his younger days, although it is doubtful if he ever played contract. When partner once appeared pained at his squandering of a king, Churchill is said to have replied, "The king cannot fall unworthily if it falls to the sword of the ace."

Mahatma Gandhi. The great Indian spiritual leader who preached the philosophy of non-violence occasionally indulged in a game of bridge and even used bridge as a metaphor to illustrate a basic Hindu belief; i.e., the difference between kharma (predetermined fate) and dharma (man's action). Kharma is the hand you are dealt. Dharma is what you do with it. And how appropriate at duplicate that you can get a good matchpoint score with a poor hand just as easily as with a good hand if you play (and bid) it correctly.

REASONS (FOR PLAYING BRIDGE)

It's an amazing game. It's difficult to take up bridge and not get passionate about it. It's so intensely gratifying when you do something right . . . and it's so maddening when you do something wrong.

— *Omar Sharif*

Undoubtedly a case could be made for the function of bridge clubs as an escape from an unbearably complicated world into the relative simplicities of what can happen with 52 cards and four people. As one player put it, "Bridge is my opium." But when you consider that 52 cards can fall into combinations that are measured in the billions even this explanation looks a little weak. For the mathematically minded, there are actually 635,013,559,600 possible hands that can come one's way.

— *Unknown*

If I had my way, I would have children taught bridge as a matter of course, just as they are taught dancing. In the end it will be more useful to them . . . you can play bridge as long as you can sit up at a table and tell one card from another. In fact, when all else fails — sports, love, ambition — bridge remains a solace and an entertainment.

— *Somerset Maugham*

We play bridge largely to build up our ego.

— *Marshall Miles*

The (duplicate bridge) group acts as a socially approved outlet for aggression.

— *Jack Stephens*

The primary reason people play tournament bridge is for the personal satisfaction of proving themselves. They are able to test themselves against excellence each time out.

— *Robert Bonomi*

Is there any more challenging, enjoyable, stimulating pastime? Chess and backgammon to mention two games which I enjoy and admire, both are splendid in their way, but they do not engage the whole personality in the way that bridge does.

— Terence Reese

You never run into the same thing. It's always different. The challenge is always there — the billions of combinations of 52 cards. The years I've played, I've never run across the same hand.

— Barry Crane

To the expert, bridge is more than a game, more than a hobby. It is the center of the universe, the beginning and end of all things physical and spiritual in life.

— Albert Morehead

That bridge is, indeed, the greatest (game) is, or rather should be, self-evident, if only because alone among card games it is absorbing enough to be played for love, without the monetary interest which gives a purpose to poker, rummy or canasta, to say nothing of baccarat or blackjack.

— Victor Mollo

People play tournament bridge for many reasons . . . (Some) play the game in order to release primitive urges; at a bridge table you can get away with actions that bear a gratifying resemblance to assault and battery, mayhem and manslaughter.

— Richard Powell, "Tickets to the Devil"

The (bridge) group acts as a microcosmic societal structure within which the individual may succeed without the advantage of money or social position. Mental dexterity determines success.

— Jack Stephens

BRIDGE Trivia Quiz

23. In what year was the American Contract Bridge League born? Answer on page 112.
24. In a survey of hundreds of tournament bridge players, one question was, "With what military campaign or historical event would you compare your most recent bridge game?" What, by far, was the most frequent answer? Answer on page 113.
25. Who was the very first life master? Answer on page 113.

Why do those who do not win continue to participate? This seems partially explainable on the basis of the desire of the group members to improve, as well as their desire to defeat the better players. Self-esteem can be won by the individual on the basis of winning in the group as a whole and in defeating the better player at any given point in the activities. It is important for the individual to defeat a "life master" on a given hand, regardless of the overall outcome.

— Jack Stephens

It would appear that a varied degree of reward satisfied the participants. The occasional reward seems to satisfy the person of known lesser ability, whereas the better players are unhappy with anything but first place. Defeating each individual appears to be equally important to those who consider themselves the better players.

— Jack Stephens

The duplicate bridge group does allow for the open demonstration of hostility and aggression in a social situation, which does not appear to happen in other social situations.

— Jack Stephens

Why be happy? Play bridge.
— *Bumper sticker*

Why do I play this game? I don't know why I play this game. I come here (to the bridge club) every night feeling good, and I go away feeling lousy. Why do I play this game? I don't know. Maybe I just enjoy torturing myself.
— *Jack Larkin in response to a fellow player's inquiry, 1976*

In no other sport or walk of life do we see the equal: top class players competing against absolute amateurs.
— *Matthew Granovetter*

Why do we play bridge anyway? For relaxation? Don't kid yourself! A good game of bridge is more exhausting than anything you do for a living.
— *Marshall Miles*

Most people play cards to waste time. Bridge players are usually suffering from an inferiority complex and find in the game an easy way to satisfy their striving for superiority.
— *Alfred Adler*

Admirable though it is to work out a game so fascinating, so difficult, so inexhaustibly novel, so dependent for its mastery on self-discipline, there is in (bridge), as in all gambling, a drunken attempt to escape from realities, and no man plays (bridge) night after night who is properly evaluating his world.
— *"The New Republic," many, many years ago*

Obscure BRIDGE Term Quiz

26. Quintract: a. a five-level contract; b. five-suited bridge; c. a tray with five compartments in which bridge refreshments are served; d. a hand on which declarer makes five overtricks or goes down five. Answer on page 113.

It is our overwhelming lust for the trivial that makes us like bridge and want to read about it.

— *"Christian Century"*

(T)he truth is that I was doing nicely in law when I simply decided to throw it all in. The law, fraught as it was with everything from petty crimes to murder, didn't seem as interesting to me as the endless permutations and combinations involved in 52 cards and four players.

— *Charles Goren*

When it comes to the noble game of bridge, I feel much the same as Talleyrand felt about the noble game of whist. The French statesman invited an aide to make a fourth, whereupon the fellow confessed that he didn't know the game. "Young man!" said Talleyrand. "You do not play whist? What a sad old age you reserve for yourself."

— *Charles Goren*

What is this fascination which bridge has for its devotees? One theory is that in bridge you can always shift the blame for your bad results, either onto the poor cards which fortune has dealt to you, or onto that poor bedevilled creature known as partner.

— *Easley Blackwood*

Bridge is more than just a card game. It is a cerebral sport. Bridge teaches you logic, reasoning, quick thinking, patience, concentration and partnership skills.

Martina Navratilova

No matter where I go, I can always make new friends at the bridge table.

— *Martina Navratilova*

You can learn to play bridge in less than six weeks — a shorter period than it would take you to learn a foreign language, and much more useful to you.

— *Peter Donovan*

There are many reasons why it's a good thing to learn bridge, but, by far and away the most important is that it's the best antidote to loneliness which has ever been invented.

— *Peter Donovan*

Bridge is more than a game. It's a passport to friendship and success in life.

— *Kathie Wei*

A well-played bridge hand has as much power to thrill and to satisfy as a Beethoven symphony.

— *Hugh Kelsey*

If people played to win money the game would have come to an end long ago, for by the nature of things, the losses must greatly exceed the gains, if only to cover the expenses. You see the same thing at duplicate. One pair wins, a few others get places, and the rest are nowhere. Yet they come up for more punishment again and again. Why? Because bridge is the medium in which they express themselves, each one doing his own thing, odd though it be.

— *The Hideous Hog*

Young people twist and ululate and disfigure themselves with pink dye. Their elders collect stocks and shares and china, or else they lecture others and join societies to inflict compassion on the poor. Those with more sense, be they young or old, boost their egos by playing bridge. Casting inhibitions to the winds, they can be crafty and cunning, scheming, hating, gloating, whining . . .

— *The Hideous Hog*

Sadism and masochism, greed and generosity, vanity and humility, all have a place. The schemer, the pedant, the psychologist, the wit, the bore, the law-giver, the anarchist, even the poet can find gratification in the pasteboard world.

— *Victor Mollo*

Bridge is first-class mental exercise and teaches more about life than Latin verbs.

— *Terence Reese*

Certainly it is worth anyone's time to become a useful bridge player. Apart from the intellectual satisfaction, he will have a hobby that never palls and a means of making friends, wherever he goes and in whatever society he moves.

— *Terence Reese*

You will find yourself transported into another world. The agitations and exacerbations of everyday life drop away from you; for awhile you dwell in a remote and austere realm of the pure intellect, uncontaminated by any practical applications; and as your game improves you may catch glimpses of some of these mathematical beauties of sequence, distribution and arrangement such as perhaps the Absolute perceives when it contemplates Itself.

— *Elmer Davis*

It offers the opportunity to conquer others. What is the inveterate card-slapper doing when he slaps down that ace but symbolically whacking his opponents in the mouth? And the player whose sole object in sitting at the table seems to be persecution of his partner? There appears to be ample evidence that far beneath the surface, bridge is used as a sledgehammer by many a player.

— *Alfred Adler*

It is almost impossible to deny that bridge is a vindictive game. Such devices as the "squeeze" and "endplay" are related in their nature to the rack and thumbscrew. Competition is a form of warfare, which by militarists, may be regarded as good sport, but which is manslaughter in one of its cruelest forms; and nowhere is the spirit of devastating competition more fiercely aroused than in contract bridge.

— *Silas Bent*

Bridge provides the opportunity to improve by competing against other players. Bridge players can enter tournaments and compete against the top experts in the game. This is a unique opportunity in competitive activities. Golfers cannot play golf against Nicklaus and tennis players cannot play tennis against Navratilova. Bridge players can sit down and compete with world and national champions.

— Mike Lawrence and Keith Hanson, from
"Winning Bridge Intangibles"

For the uninitiated, there are two reasons why bridge is endlessly fascinating. There is no conquering it. No matter how much one improves, no matter how hard one works at it, there are new heights to scale, new layers to unfold, new dimensions to discover. It endlessly renews itself. No other game produces the endless variations that bridge does.

— Joyce Nicholson

All-Animal BRIDGE Team

1. David BIRD
2. Barry CRANE
3. Charles COON
4. Ed CHOW
5. G. C. H. FOX
6. Ralph KATZ
7. Mrs. Ruby LYONS
8. Bobby WOLFF
9. Chuck LAMPREY
10. Dr. Nathan OSTRICH
11. Mrs. L. B. SWAN
12. Henry BAER
13. Ross ROBBINS
14. Leonard KARP

There are people who have no head for cards. It is impossible not to be sorry for them, for what, one asks oneself, can the future have to offer them when the glow of youth has departed and advancing years force them, as they force all of us, to be spectators rather than actors in the comedy of life? Love is for the young and affection is but a frigid solace to a pining heart. Sport demands physical vigour and affairs a strenuous activity. To have learnt to play a good game of bridge is the safest insurance against the tedium of old age. Throughout life one may find in cards endless entertainment and an occupation for idle hours that rests the mind from care and pleasantly exercises the intelligence. For the people who say that only the stupid can play cards err; they do not know what decision, what quickness of apprehension, what judgment, what knowledge of character, are required to play a difficult hand perfectly. The good card player trusts his intuition as implicitly as Monsieur Bergson, but he calls it a hunch; the brilliant card player has a gift as specific as the poet's; he too is born not made. The student of human nature can find endless matter for observation in the behaviour of his fellow card players. Meanness and generosity, prudence and audacity, courage and timidity, weakness and strength; all these men show at the card table according to their nature, and because they are intent upon the game drop the mask they wear in the ordinary affairs of life. Few are so deep that you do not know the essential facts about them after a few rubbers of bridge. The card table is a very good school for the study of mankind . . .

— From the General Introduction by
W. Somerset Maugham to his
"Traveller's Library"

BRIDGE Trivia Quiz

27. Assuming no revokes, but the most favorable lie of the cards, what is the minimum high card count you can have and still be cold for a grand slam in spades? Answer on page 113.

Universal Laws of BRIDGE

- When the opponents bid a 10 percent slam, they end up with a plus score. When you bid a 90 percent slam, the opponents also end up with a plus score.
- In a tough bidding situation, if there is one interpretation that partner couldn't possible place on your bid, that is the interpretation he will place on your bid.
- On a hand where everyone else should get into the same trouble, no one does.
- When you lose, it is bad luck. When you win, it is skill.
- And yes, it's ALWAYS partner's fault.

So why do we play bridge? The answer is simple, right? We play because it's fun; it's an intellectual challenge . . . Right? Wrong! At least, these ideas are wrong according to the many "experts" who have plumbed the depth of the national psyche to find out where the steam of bridge is boilered. Bridge, it turns out, is not fun; it's a chore, a way of evading life, a means of ventilating deep hostilities and supercharging dull, unrewarding lives with a phony stimulation.

— Jack Olsen

Bridge is for fun. You should play the game for no other reason. You should not play bridge to make money, to show how smart you are, or show how stupid your partner is . . . or to prove any of the several hundred other things bridge players are so often trying to prove.

— Charles Goren

You should play the game for fun. The instant you find yourself playing the game for any other reason, you should rack it up and go on to something else . . .

— Charles Goren

One night I was kibitizing a big tournament. After watching play for a couple of hours, I realized that three quarters of the people there were *not* playing bridge. Oh, they thought they were. But for the most part they were not there to play bridge. Or, to put it another way, they were playing bridge, but playing bridge was not the real reason they were there. Some of them had fallen for one of the new gimmick systems and were spending the evening baffling opponents and partners alike with bids that nobody understands and which, if understood, would not have been wise bids anyway. This is not bridge, it is mnemonics. Then there were the usual tyrannical players blowing their tops at partners who had failed to return their leads. That is not bridge; it is sadism. And their partners would sit patiently and take all this abuse. This is not bridge; it is masochism.

— *Charles Goren*

Nobody plays duplicate bridge only for pleasure.
— *Anonymous tournament player*

If serenity is one's major ambition, perhaps bridge should be avoided.
— *Charles Goren*

Playing bridge reflects intelligence. It's one of the really great pleasures of life. I think anybody who's missing bridge is missing so much in life. Don't make the mistake of missing out on the fun of bridge.
— *Malcolm Forbes*

If you have the slightest touch of masochism, you'll love this game.
— *Advice offered to a kibitzer who explained that she didn't know how to play the game but wanted to learn*

The more complex the mind, the greater the need for the simplicity of play.
— *Mr. Spock on "Star Trek"*

REVIEWS

You may ask where you are, but not how you got there.
— *Tournament director, Jerry Machlin,*
ruling that once play has begun,
declarer may ask what the contract
is, but not for a review of the auction

REVOKES

When you can't follow suit, follow color — especially late in the game.

— *Alfred Sheinwold*

SCIENTIFIC BIDDING

Successful bridge is not the result of precise, scientific bidding. On the contrary good scores usually result from contracts that have been reached in less than three rounds of bidding. The fewer bids you take to reach a contract, the higher your score. The failure to recognize this concept is a major stumbling block to most duplicate players, who were taught erroneously that scientific bidding is the key to success.

— *Matthew Granovetter*

SEX

I have sold bridge through sex — the game brought men and women together. I used the words "forcing bid" and "approach bid" because there is a connotation of sex to them.

— *Ely Culbertson*

In its effect on men and women, bridge is not an erotic pastime. Compared to it, such activities as dancing the waltz, playing mixed doubles in tennis and holding hands during a walk must be rated as orgies.

— *Richard Powell*

In the course of a serious bridge game, men and women excite each other sexually about as often as they hold a Yarborough, a hand in which no card is higher than a nine. The odds against a Yarborough are 1,827 to one.

— *Richard Powell*

I always play best after I've spent a hot night in bed with a lovely girl.

— *Zia Mahmood*

Famous BRIDGE Players

Deng Xiao-Ping: The leader of Red China was honored by the International Bridge Press Association as bridge personality of the year in 1980, although he has been playing the game for decades, even during personally far less successful times when his frequent indulgence in this "decadent Western pastime" was offered as evidence of improper bourgeois attitudes.

Deng Xiao-Ping was a victim of the purges during Mao Tse-Tung's Cultural Revolution in the late 1960's. As a headline in the *New York Times* in March of 1967 proclaimed: "Anti-Mao leader is accused of too much bridge playing."

Among Deng's alleged derelictions were using state building materials and funds to construct a fancy club where he and his cronies played bridge. According to a Red Guard newspaper at the time, "This club, with elaborate facilities for eating, drinking and games, became Mr. Deng's bridge hangout where he enlisted capitulationsists and renegades and gathered together demons and monsters." Officials allegedly had to interrupt the bridge game to get Deng to put his "stinking signature" on important papers.

When on tours out of Peking, Deng was accused of arranging for his bridge playing companions to go with him so he could always have partners for a game, of traveling in a special railway car where bridge games went on constantly, and even of getting bored on a work trip to Manchuria and flying his bridge friends in on a special plane.

All his bridge buddies were purged, too.

"He (Deng) has been paraded through Peking's streets wearing a dunce cap and a placard labeling him a counterrevoluntionary," reported *Tung Fang Hung,* a Peking tabloid newspaper, in early 1967.

In more recent years, Deng Xiao-Ping has promoted bridge playing in his country and fostered international competition. The People's Republic of China recently became a member of the World Bridge Federation.

SKILL VS. LUCK

The primary reason for the widespread interest in contract bridge is the fact that the game combines the elements of 'skill' and 'luck' in the most palatable proportion; it has been estimated by various authorities that 'skill' comprises about 65 percent while 'luck' is about 35 percent. In order for a game to rise to the plane of universal popularity, it must possess these two essential ingredients. But should a game have too much luck attached to it (as dice, for example), the stimulation and incentive to the player's skill are not sufficient to sustain his interest. On the other hand, should a game require too much thought and skill — as chess — the poorer player will turn to something else which will give him a better chance to excel. It is unquestionably the harmonious combination of skill and luck which has served to hold the interest of contract bridge's millions of disciples.

— Fred Karpin

SLOW PLAY

I must have spent six years of my life waiting for other people to finish games.

— Oswald Jacoby

A card must be played the same day it is dealt.

— Anonymous

I was a young man when it started.

— Lee Hazen, asking for a review in the 1956 World Championships after the French took 23 minutes to get to the wrong contract

(T)here is (a) kind of slow player, deliberately devious, who uses the delaying ploy in a kind of cunning war of nerves. He does not give a damn how many people are waiting behind him or how many "late play" penalties are created because of him. He bids and plays at the pace of a turtle, and I call these players "volitional catatonics." One Sunday I played against a young man who, I learned later, was a notorious time-killer. Whenever it came his turn to play a card, he would stare blankly into space for two or three minutes before exposing his card. In one particular hand, he held onto a worthless deuce of clubs for five minutes. The way he sat and pondered, I thought he was making some profoundly deep decision — like whether unilateral disarmament could avoid nuclear war. The club director had long since called the move, and still my opponent sat spaced-out over his deuce of clubs. The result of his slowness was to cause my partner and me to fall behind for the rest of the afternoon and ultimately take a "late play." I was very irritated by this, and I mentioned my annoyance to one of the experienced players. I said to her, "My God, what was he pondering about? While he sat dithering for five full minutes, I got so bored and restless that I forgot every card that had been played, and I lost control of the hand." She smiled patiently. "But that was precisely his purpose," she said.

— *Fleur Tamon, "The Houston Post"*

The History of BRIDGE

Contract Bridge: This modern version of bridge was invented in 1925 by Harold S. Vanderbilt. The method of scoring changes somewhat (with the concept of vulnerability being introduced) but the major change is in the bidding. Bidding becames more important because now in order to get credit for a game or slam, it must be bid.

The slowpoke cannot be mistaken for anything else. Its hard shell is impervious to murmers of impatience. The firmly compressed mouth, the astigmatic eye, the tentative phalanges — all these mark the studiously deliberate beast. Will the slowpoke bid? Yes, but not until its hand has been sorted, resorted, opened, closed, opened again, breasted, chested, counted and recounted, and thoughtfully appraised. "Pass," says the slowpoke at last, thus opening the auction. The slowpoke is looking at one naked ace and two red jacks. Such difficult bids plainly require a great deal of time.

— *James Kilpatrick*

It takes her an hour and a half to watch "Sixty Minutes."
— *One player speaking of a slow teammate*

SOCIAL SKILL (BRIDGE AS A)

There are people who have no head for cards. It is impossible not to be sorry for them, for what, one asks one's self, can the future offer them when the glow of youth has departed and advancing years force them, as they force all of us, to be spectators rather than actors in the comedy of life. To have learned to play a good game of bridge is the safest insurance against the tedium of old age. Throughout life one might find in cards endless entertainment and occupation for idle hours that rests the mind and exercises the intelligence.

— *Somerset Maugham*

If I had my way, I would have children taught bridge as a matter of course, just as they are taught dancing. In the end it will be more useful to them . . . you can play bridge as long as you can sit up at a table and tell one card from another. In fact, when all else fails — sport, love, ambition — bridge remains a solace and an entertainment.

— *Somerset Maugham*

Here's a most interesting fact about bridge — you're never alone anywhere in the world when you're a bridge player. It's like having a special passport. You can go into a strange town, ask where the bridge game is, and immediately you're able to cut in for a rubber or two. Or if there's a duplicate game, the club manager will always go out of his way to find a partner for you.

— Unknown

Social occasions are only warfare concealed.

— Khan on "Star Trek"

SPORTSMANSHIP

I deplore all this pseudo sportsmanship. It's undignified. One doesn't cheer at billiards when a player doesn't miscue or at tennis when someone gets the ball over the net. Why, then, should one pat partner on the back every time he counts correctly up to thirteen?

— The Hideous Hog

SWINDLES

It's not enough to win the tricks that belong to you. Try also for some that belong to the opponents.

— Alfred Sheinwold

TOURNAMENT BRIDGE

That is not a game at all, but a miniature battle played with cards and dirty looks instead of guns and bayonets.

— An anonymous writer calling himself
"Ely Lenz"

TOURNAMENT PLAYERS

They are on some sort of ego trip.

— *Bob Hamman*

WHIST

Take this simple game, add a dummy, the concept of notrump bidding, and an occasional felonious assault, and you have contract bridge.

— *Jack Olsen*

WINNING

The real test of a bridge player isn't in keeping out of trouble, but in escaping once he's in.

— *Alfred Sheinwold*

Are you sure the computer didn't misadd our score by a hundred points?

— *Peter Weichsel, upon hearing that he and Alan Sontag had won the Life Masters Pairs at the 1977 Summer North American Championships in Chicago*

Obscure BRIDGE Term Quiz

28. Vint: a. an exotic three-suited progressive squeeze; b. to force declarer to ruff so many times he loses control of the hand; c. another term for revoke at whist; d. a Russian game similar to bridge.
29. Younger: a. opening leader's partner; b. the youngest player in the game; c. the most inexperienced player in the game; d. the opening leader. Answers on page 113.

Winning in bridge, just as in many other challenges, involves a state of mind. If you believe you are going to lose, you probably will. If you really believe you are going to win, you usually will. Somehow, when you are in the winning confident state of mind, you will appear to become a lucky player. Actually, you are playing better and taking advantage of the opportunities.

— Anonymous

Winning may not be everything, but as Charlie Brown . . . is wont to observe, losing isn't anything.

— Allan Falk

No person was ever proven a better human being for having won a bridge tournament or a lesser one for having lost one.

— Frank Queen

There is too much stress everywhere on the art of winning and not nearly enough anywhere on the art of losing.

— Victor Mollo

Greed is good, greed is right, greed works.

— Gordon Gekko in "Wall Street"

If winning is not important, then tell me, why keep score?

— Klingon crew member in "Star Trek, the Next Generation"

Whoever said, "It's not whether you win or lose that counts," probably lost.

— Martina Navratilova

WOMEN

Most women are so remarkably illogical.
— A well-known bridge writer

Women! Don't talk to me about women bridge players. They are hopeless. They don't concentrate properly. They are too busy gazing around the room. They're always looking here, looking there. Not looking at the cards. Thinking about clothes, and people, and parties, instead of thinking about the cards.
— Rixi Markus

The trouble with women is that they treat bridge as a game. They do not realize it is a war.
— Anonymous

Men see bridge as a battle which they have to win.
Women are not prepared to cut a friend's throat for an overtrick.
Women lack the killer instinct.
The drive to win is much stronger in men.
Women are not tough enough.
Women do not take games seriously.
Men are taught to be more aggressive from birth.
Women treat bridge as a game, men know it is not.
Women can't compete.
Women do not have the will to win.
— Answers to a questionnaire on why women are not as successful at bridge as men

---

Some authorities favor India over China as the original source of playing cards.

Cards reached England later than the rest of Europe with the earliest clear-cut references dating from 1465.

The modern bridge or poker deck probably derived from the early Italian tarot packs.

Men are better bridge players than women. (Women) haven't got the killer instinct.

— Stan Tench, tournament director

Women are not aggressive enough. They don't compete enough in the bidding. They don't make aggressive leads. They play too passively.

— Anonymous

The worst verbal abuses are nearly always men against women, and it must affect the women's game.

— Joyce Nicholson

Women who seek pre-eminence at bridge are disadvantaged in a number of ways, just as they are in other fields of endeavor.

— Hugh Kelsey

Men are better at bridge because they are better at anything.

— A leading bridge writer as quoted
by Joyce Nicholson in "Why Women
Lose at Bridge"

Women are better — men are best!

— Alfred Sheinwold, once asked at a
bridge teacher's convention how he
compared men and women bridge
players

Women are more intelligent. The proof? You will never find them devoting all their time and energy to mastering so trivial a subject as bridge. So how can you expect them to play as well as men?

— Omar Sharif

A woman's inner sense of value tells her that bridge is not really a matter of life and death, but a man, whose ego is at stake, is a much harder fighter and treats bridge as a challenge to his mentality.

— Anonymous

If women devoted as much time to bridge as men, the basic unit of society, the family, would be adversely affected, and we would have a generation of children brought up without maternal care . . . it is not that women are inferior.

— Anonymous

There is no wonder women do not reach the top in what is a fiercely competitive game . . . women are taught to be acquiescent . . . these characteristics are induced as early as the cradle and reinforced by sexual stereotypes in society and at school.

— David Askew

Men are brought up to be ambitious and women to focus on other things.

— A. Boekhurst

Women are taught not to be competitive.

— Svend Novrup

Women are not encouraged by society to use their intelligence in business or mental sports.

— Michael Becker

Women are less suited by training for a competitive and intelligent game.

— James Jacoby

Women have not been brought up to challenge so keenly.

— *David Brown*

Women do not neglect their children and family to play in a tournament. It would be better if men were less fanatical and neglectful. They should be equalized down rather than women moving toward male attitudes.

— *Alfred Sheinwold*

One reason women find the game of bridge more difficult, I think, is that their minds are not always logical. On the whole, women are inclined to think with emotion . . . but bridge is a game of logic.

— *Rixi Markus*

Because men have mental stimulation at work, their minds remain more disciplined.

— *Anonymous*

There are many reasons for women's lack of concentration (at the bridge table) and they are mainly concerned with children. By bringing up children many woman actually lose their ability to concentrate. It is the daily and constant contact with small children that fragments a woman's concentration.

— *Joyce Nicholson*

Women do not strive for perfection, so are not so rude, they accept error.

— *Anonymous*

Quiz Answers

8. 4-4-3-2, 5-3-3-2 and 5-4-3-1. (Question on page 30.)
9. The probabilities are equally likely. If you and your partner hold no clubs, then your opponents hold all the clubs. (Question on page 30.)
10. A (Question on page 34.)
11. B (Question on page 48.)
12. Nine (Question on page 55.)

Another factor that causes men to downgrade women's bridge is that with a mixed partnership, the man tends to think he is better, takes control, does not trust his partner in regard to leading and bidding, and thus often plays bad bridge. Then, when failure results, he blames her.

— *Joyce Nicholson*

As bridge became more professional, more deadly earnest, more a war and less a game, more a means of earning a living, it is possible that men, who run this world, subconsciously decided it was time for women to be banished from the top echelons.

— *Joyce Nicholson*

To be honest, when a man and woman play and travel together regularly, other players do tend to think they sleep together.

— *Joyce Nicholson*

I side with the psychologists in claiming that women are more emotional than men. They tend to be guided by instinct rather than logic . . . and nowhere, except perhaps in the driver's seat of a car, is this ascendancy of feeling over thought more manifest than at the bridge table. A woman's course of play may be affected by quite irrelevant and entirely personal emotions — she may strive to outbid an opponent for no better reason than that she envies her hat — or her husband . . .

— *Anonymous (but the author of that passage was a woman)*

A killer instinct is needed to reach the top. You need the will to win. Many women, God bless them, are fine bridge players but lack this competitive fire, often because they learned bridge in a social setting. That's why you see mostly men at the top.

— *Peter Pender*

Quiz Answers

13. "When the king is singleton play the ace." (Question on page 55.)
14. The deuce of clubs. (Question on page 55.)
15. 7,600, for down 13, redoubled and vulnerable. (Question on page 55.)
16. C (Question on page 61.)
17. A (Question on page 61.)
18. A term indicating either the queen or jack in situations where it is of no consequence which of the two cards is held or played. (Question on page 76.)
19. The nine of diamonds. (Question on page 76.)
20. Goldwater's Rule: A player who does not know whose lead it is probably doesn't know what to lead either. (Question on page 76.)

Bridge is one of the few pastimes in which a woman is on a footing of equality with a man, and may even show him a trick or two. This would fortify women against their natural sense of inferiority.

— *Ely Culbertson on publicizing bridge*

Women make better players than men. They do not mind defeat as much. Men hate to be beaten.

— *Ira Corn*

You can't be a lady. You've got to hate everybody you play against. You have got to be a killer whether you like it or not.

— *Tobias Stone teaching his wife to play bridge*

The dearth of top-notch female players is often attributed to the need for cold cruelty in play, a cold cruelty which men have had in their genes since paleolithic days and women have by and large repressed.

— *Jack Olsen*

One dictionary defines a basilisk as a fabulous creature with black-and-yellow skin and fierce death-dealing eyes and breath. This definition provokes the thought that the lexicographer had never frequented a women's bridge club, or he would have otherwise omitted the word "fabulous."

— *Rex Mackey*

The truth of the matter is that when playing cards women cannot help a facial expression which would freeze the libidinous ardor of the great god Pan himself, for their predatory anxiety makes them bad winners and worse losers.

— *Rex Mackey*

It is a matter of fact . . . that the only two players charged with committing murder at the bridge table were women. Apart from Mrs. Bennett, Mrs. Henderson of Detroit, Michigan, had the misfortune to play with a partner who pulled the wrong card twice in succession. She expressed her vexation in the only possible way by shooting the lady accurately between the eyes.

— *Rex Mackey*

First we had to build a system. That took six years. Then we had to sell the system. We appealed to women, to their natural inferiority complex.

— *Ely Culbertson*

Quiz Answers

21. Green. Hippogriffs are a mythical suit in an anecdote where a man thought he had a perfect seven notrump in hand. He was set by the devil who cashed 13 tricks by running a weird greenish suit called hippogriffs. (Question on page 76.)
22. B (Question on page 85.)
23. 1937 (question on page 89.)

24. Waterloo (Question on page 89.)
25. David Bruce (Question on page 89.)
26. B (Question on page 90.)
27. 5 (Question on page 95.)
28. D (Question on page 104.)
29. A (Question on page 104.)

Bridge was an opportunity for them (women) to gain intellectual parity with this husbands. We worked on their fear instincts. We made it almost tantamount to shame not to play contract.

— *Ely Culbertson*

The role of the differences in sex with the (duplicate bridge) group appears to be somewhat unusual. Although a large majority of the players are female, the greatest players are usually men. Is there some factor in the background of the different sexes which leads to greater or lesser success at the game? Does the male have more of the "killer instinct" generally conceded to be necessary in the great players, or does he merely have more of the stamina necessary in a grueling tournament which lasts eight or nine days?

— *Jack Stephens*

Although there have been several women who are acknowledged to be the equal of their male contemporaries, the fact is that in general men are better at bridge than women. This is an unpopular view, yet the evidence for it is overwhelming . . .

— *Rixi Markus*

QUOTED IN
"CLASSIC BRIDGE QUOTES"

ALFRED ADLER: publisher, philosopher

DAVID ASKEW: Australian bridge writer.

RON ANDERSEN: national expert, number two masterpoint holder in the U.S.

MARY BAPTIST: Denver area bridge player.

GRANT BAZE: national expert, set record for most masterpoints won in a single year.

MICHAEL BECKER: national expert.

MARTHA BEECHER: national expert.

SILAS BENT: bridge writer.

GEORGE BEYNON: authority on tournament direction.

EASLEY BLACKWOOD: top player and writer, inventor of Blackwood convention.

A. BOEKHURST: Dutch bridge writer,

ROBERT BONOMI: ACBL publicist, 1970's and early 1980's.

DAVID BROWN: British bridge writer.

WARREN BUFFETT: businessman, investor.

PAUL BURKA: editor, Texas Monthly.

CAVENDISH: pseudonym of Henry Jones, a London whist authority.

BEN COHEN: bridge writer, early pioneer of duplicate.

IRA CORN: captain of Dallas Aces.

BILL COSBY: comedian.

BARRY CRANE: all-time top masterpoint holder, murdered in 1985.

JOHN CRAWFORD: top player and writer.

ELY CULBERTSON: one of the first great players, author of the Culbertson system.

ELMER DAVIS: bridge writer.

PETER DONOVAN: British player and writer.

ROBERT EWEN: top player and writer.

ALLAN FALK: top player and writer.

BOBBY FISCHER: world chess champion.

CATHERINE FORD: Canadian journalist.

MALCOLM FORBES: American businessman and entrepreneur.

RICHARD FREY: top player and writer.

SAM FRY: top player and writer.

CHARLES GOREN: top player, writer, columnist, author of the Goren system.

CLYDE GRAHAM: Denver area bridge player.

MATTHEW GRANOVETTER: national expert and bridge author, co-editor of *Bridge Today*.

ROBERT HAMMAN: world champion.

KEITH HANSON: bridge author and teacher.

MAX HARDY: top player, director, publisher and writer.

GAREY HAYDEN: national expert.

LEE HAZEN: top player and writer.

CHUCK HENKE: Denver area bridge player.

GEORGE HERVEY: British writer.

HIDEOUS HOG: character in Victor Mollo's *Menagerie* series.

TANNAH HIRSCH: top player and writer.

PAUL HOFFMAN: writer.

ZEKE JABBOUR: national expert.

MARC JACOBUS: national expert.

JAMES JACOBY: national expert, syndicated columnist.

OSWALD JACOBY: one of the country's all-time top players and bridge writers, winner of a major championship in all decades from 20's to 80's.

JAN JANITSCHKE: national expert.

EDDIE KANTAR: national expert and writer.

EDGAR KAPLAN: national expert and writer, editor of *Bridge World*.

FRED KARPIN: top player and writer.

GAYLOR KASLE: national expert.

GEORGE KAUFMAN: top player and writer.

NORMAN KAY: national expert and writer.

H. W. KELSEY: top Scottish player and writer.

EWART KEMPSON: editor, *Bridge Magazine.*

JAMES KILPATRICK: political writer.

RON KLINGER: Australian bridge writer.

CHARLES LAMB: English essayist.

JACK LARKIN: Rocky Mountain bridge player.

MIKE LAWRENCE: world champion and bridge writer.

JOSE LE DENTU: top French player and writer.

RICHARD LEDERER: the first great figure in British bridge, writer.

SIDNEY LENZ: top player in the 1930's.

PAUL LEWIS: national expert.

REX MACKEY: bridge writer.

ZIA MAHMOOD: top international player from Pakistan.

RIXI MARKUS: top English player.

CHIP MARTEL: world champion.

CHICO MARX: comedian.

SOMERSET MAUGHAM: English writer.

EDWARD MAYER: British player and writer.

H. L. MENCKEN: American journalist.

MARSHALL MILES: top player and writer.

VICTOR MOLLO: English bridge writer.

ALBERT MOREHEAD: bridge writer and theoretician.

MARTINA NAVRATILOVA: world tennis champion.

JOYCE NICHOLSON: Australian bridge writer.

SVEND NOVRUP: Norwegian bridge writer,

DON OAKIE: national expert.

JACK OLSEN: bridge humorist and historian.

FLORENCE OSBORN: bridge columnist.

ALBERT OSTROW: bridge writer.

MILTON OZAKI: bridge writer.

PETER PENDER: world champion.

PEREGRINE THE PENGUIN: one of Victor Mollo's *Menagerie* characters.

EDGAR ALLEN POE: U. S. short story writer.

RICHARD POWELL: novelist.

FRANK QUEEN: Denver area bridge player, unit president.

R. R. RICHARDS: first president of American Bridge League.

TERENCE REESE: top English player and writer.

HAROLD ROCKAWAY: psychiatrist, top player.

ERIC RODWELL: world champion.

GEORGE ROSENKRANZ: top Mexican player and writer.

ERNEST ROVERE: bridge writer, columnist for San Francisco Chronicle.

RUEFUL RABBIT: one of Victor Mollo's *Menagerie* characters.

HOWARD SCHENKEN: top player and writer.

JEAN-PAUL SARTRE: French philosopher.

JIM SCOTT: Denver area bridge player.

LOIS SCOTT: Denver area bridge player.

OMAR SHARIF: actor and bridge player, co-author of *Goren on Bridge.*

ALFRED SHEINWOLD: syndicated bridge columnist.

PAUL SIMON: Pop singer-songwriter.

S. J. SIMON: British bridge writer.

HAL SIMS: top player in the 1930's, took part in famous Sims-Culbertson match.

JERRY SOHL: bridge writer.

PAUL SOLOWAY: top masterpoint holder in U.S.

ALAN SONTAG: national expert.

FRANK STEWART: top player and bridge writer, editor of *Contract Bridge Bulletin.*

NORMAN SQUIRE: British bridge writer.

TOBIAS STONE: top player and co-inventor of Roth-Stone system.

ROBERT SUNDBY: bridge author.

JONATHAN SWIFT: English author.

TALLEYRAND: French statesman.

FLEUR TAMON: journalist.

STAN TENCH: tournament director.

ALAN TRUSCOTT: bridge editor, *New York Times*.

FRANK VINE: bridge writer.

PETER WEICHSEL: national expert.

KATHIE WEI: national expert, major promoter of Precision system.

OSCAR WILDE: English writer.

THE TEN COMMANDMENTS OF BRIDGE

Do you have a bridge partner who generally plays a pretty steady game, but who occasionally does something bizarre at the bridge table, resulting in a disaster that cancels out all the good hands? Mail him or her an anonymous copy of The Ten Commandments of Bridge:

I. Thou shalt not pull thy partner's high-level penalty doubles — ever!

II. Thou shalt not double thy opponents' partscore contract without four sure trump tricks; if thou doublest thy opponents' game contract, thou shalt make the killing lead.

III. If thy partner maketh a low-level double and thou art uncertain as to whether it is for penalty, takeout or reopening, thou shalt bid again.

IV. Thou shalt not miss cold games; thou shalt not sac against a game that doesn't make.

V. Thou shalt not bid 10% slams; thou shalt not bid seven notrump off an ace.

VI. Thou shalt not make vulnerable overcalls on king-ten-fifth; thou shalt not rebid thy king-empty-sixth suit three times.

VII. Thou shalt not go on a drinking binge between sessions.

VIII. Thou shalt not go for numbers.

IX. Thou shalt not lead out of turn.

X. Thou shalt not revoke.

HOW TO BE A POPULAR KIBITZER

Everybody likes to be popular. Want to make a name for yourself as a kibitzer at the bridge table? Here are 10 easy suggestions:

1. Don't be satisfied with kibitzing just one hand. Wander around. Circulate. When you spot a bad hand, yawn to let everyone know about it, then find a hand with more high cards to kibitz.
2. Don't be afraid to speak up. Be sure to make some snide comment about the bidding or play on each hand. The other four players will be disappointed if they don't hear from you. When sitting behind declarer, be sure to mumble "tch, tch" (be sure it's audible) when he goes down in his contract, even if it was a profitable sacrifice. And even if the contract was impossible to make, be sure to suggest, "I don't think you can make it, but you can give yourself a better play."
3. When sitting behind an opening leader who has spent five minutes pondering his lead and finally selected his card with confidence, shake your head in disgust no matter what he leads.
4. Every time declarer miscounts trumps and gets an unexpected ruff at trick 11, be sure to chuckle.
5. Whenever declarer makes a doubled partscore, rub your hands together and say something like, "Let's see, three spades, doubled, making five. How much IS that? Let's see, 50 for the insult . . ." The opponents will appreciate your helpfulness.
6. When the opponents fail to bid a cold slam, be sure to remind them that if they were playing the system you play, it would have been easy to get to. Offer to explain it to them. When they decline, explain it to them anyway.
7. Don't get stuck turning the dummy.

8. Refuse to fetch coffee, beer or soft drinks for anyone. Always point to the current dummy and say, "He's not doing anything right now. He can do it."

9. Ask the players how much they're playing for and whatever stakes you're told, let out with a contemptuous snort.

10. Whenever the opportunity arises, be sure to brag about the world champions you've had the opportunity to kibitz; you know, REAL bridge. The other players will appreciate the comparison.

Oh yes, one other thing. Keep your eye on the door, should you need to make a fast exit.

DEVYN PRESS PUBLICATIONS
BRIDGE BOOKS

BARON-STEWART:
The Bridge Student Text —
Vol. 1, for Beginning Players 4.95
Vol. 2, for Intermediate Players 4.95
Vol. 3, for Advanced Players 4.95
Vol. 4, Defensive Play 4.95
The Bridge Teachers' Manual —
Vol. 1, for Beginning Players 11.95
Vol. 2, for Intermediate Players 11.95
Vol. 3, for Advanced Players 11.95
Vol. 4, Defensive Play 11.95
BARON-WOOLSEY:
Clobber Their Artificial Club 2.95
BERNSTEIN-BARON:
Do You Know Your Partner? 1.95
BLACKWOOD:
Complete Book of Opening Leads 12.95
BLACKWOOD-HANSON:
Card Play Fundamentals 5.95
EBER-FREEMAN:
Have I Got a Story for You 7.95
FLANNERY:
The Flannery 2◇ Convention 7.95
GOODWIN:
Table Talk 5.95
Let's Play Cards: Great Card Games
for Children 9.95
GORSKI:
Art of Logical Bidding 4.95
HARRIS:
Bridge Director's Companion 12.95
HARRISON:
Player's Guide to the Rules of Duplicate Bridge . 9.95
JOHNSON:
Classic Bridge Quotes 6.95
KEARSE:
Bridge Conventions Complete 17.95
KELSEY:
Countdown to Better Bridge 9.95
101 Bridge Maxims 7.95
LAWRENCE:
How to Play Card Combinations 9.95
Dynamic Defense 9.95
Falsecards 9.95
How to Read the Opponents' Cards 7.95
Partnership Understandings 2.95
Play Bridge with Mike Lawrence 9.95
LAWRENCE-HANSON:
Winning Bridge Intangibles 2.95
PENICK:
Beginning Bridge Complete 6.95
Beginning Bridge Quizzes 6.95
POWELL:
Tickets to the Devil 5.95
REESE:
Play These Hands With Me 7.95
REESE-HOFFMAN:
Play It Again, Sam 7.95

ROSENKRANZ:
The Bidder's Game 12.95
Everything You Ever Wanted to
Know About Trump Leads 7.95
Tips for Tops 9.95
ROSENKRANZ-TRUSCOTT:
Modern Ideas in Bidding 9.95
RUBENS-LUKACS:
Test Your Play as Declarer, Vol. 1, ... 5.95
SHEINWOLD:
Bridge Puzzles, Vol. 1 . . . . 5.95
Bridge Puzzles, Vol. 2 . . . . 4.95
Bridge Puzzles, Vol. 3 . . . . 4.95
STEWART-BARON:
The Bridge Book
Vol. 1, for Beginning Players 7.95
Vol. 2, for Intermediate Players 7.95
Vol. 3, for Advanced Players 7.95
Vol. 4, Defensive Play 7.95
WOLFF:
Bidding Challenge 6.95
WOOLSEY:
Matchpoints 9.95
Partnership Defense 8.95

BRIDGE COMPUTER PROGRAMS
Mike Lawrence's Bridge Dealer
(IBM or Macintosh) 50.00
Tournament Bridge (IBM or Apple) 49.95

BRIDGE FLASHCARDS
TRUSCOTT-GORDY:
Standard Plays of Card Combinations 6.95

BRIDGE PAMPHLETS
Championship Bridge Series —
Volume 1 (#1-12) 9.95
Volume 2 (#13-24) 9.95
Volume 3 (#25-36) 9.95
Future Champions' Bridge Series —
Volume 1 (#1-12) 9.95
Hanson: Fingertip Bridge 95
Keenan: Roman Key Card Blackwood 95
Stewart-Baron: How To Be A Good Partner 95

SPORTS TITLES
BARON-VON BORRIES:
Official Ky. Derby Quiz Book 11.95
BARON-RICE:
Official U. of Ky. Basketball Book 9.95
HILL-BARON:
The Amazing Basketball Book 8.95